REGIONAL PAYMENTS MECHANISMS:
THE CASE OF PUERTO RICO

REGIONAL PAYMENTS MECHANISMS:
THE CASE OF PUERTO RICO

by

JAMES C. INGRAM

THE UNIVERSITY OF NORTH CAROLINA PRESS

Chapel Hill

332.15
IN4r
88138
april 1974

PREFACE

This study grew out of an earlier interest in the process
through which state and regional balances of payments are
adjusted within the continental United States. The lack
of data for estimation of balances of payments for a state
or region has led to several attempts to use the data on
regional flows of funds, as collected and issued by the
Interdistrict Settlement Fund of the Federal Reserve
System, for the analysis of regional adjustments. However, it soon became apparent that these data were not
much help. In this study I have treated Puerto Rico as a
region of the United States, and I have sought to analyze
the process of adjustment in the Puerto Rican balance of
payments in the hope that something would be learned
about regional payments mechanisms within the United
States, and perhaps even about payments mechanisms in a
customs union such as the European Economic Community.

Although this is a study of regional payments adjustments, the approach and method of analysis is that of
international economics. I treat Puerto Rico as if she
were a nation and make use of international trade analogies throughout the book.

This book contains three separate but closely related
parts. First, it contains estimates of the gross flows of
funds to and from Puerto Rico for three fiscal years, 1958,
1959, and 1960. These flows are analogous to the flows of
funds among Federal Reserve districts, but the Puerto
Rican data are superior in several respects. The basis and
method of estimation are described in Chapter II and its
appendix. Second, Chapters III-V contain an analysis of
Puerto Rico's postwar balance-of-payments experience.
Since 1946 Puerto Rico has received a massive inflow of

capital, and I have attempted to analyze the mechanism of response to this capital inflow. This analysis utilizes the excellent statistics of gross product and balance of payments published by the Planning Board. It was the existence of these data, published regularly on a consistent basis, that made this study possible.

Third, in Chapter VI, I have attempted to explain why Puerto Rico is not troubled by balance-of-payments problems in the same sense that nations are, and I have suggested some implications of this study for the payments mechanism in a customs union or in any group of nations whose economies are closely integrated. These implications are highly tentative, as we are here examining only part of the whole problem. However, I hope the suggested implications will prove relevant to recent discussions of proposals for international monetary reform.

A great many people have generously given me advice and assistance in the course of this study. The estimates of external flows of funds could never have been made without the help and cooperation of Puerto Rican commercial banks, the United States Treasury Department, and several branches of the Commonwealth government, especially the Planning Board, Treasury Department, and public authorities. I regret that I cannot list all of the persons to whom I am indebted, but I wish particularly to acknowledge my debt to Mrs. Edna Ranck, Alvin Mayne, and Alberto Morales of the Commonwealth Planning Board; Webster Pullen of the First National City Bank of New York; and H. A. Rabon, Jr., of the United States Treasury Department. I also wish to thank Dr. Mohinder Bhatia, David S. Ball, and Gary Hyde for their careful comments on a draft version of this study, and Professor Tibor Scitovsky for reading Chapter VI.

Research in Puerto Rico during the spring and summer of 1960 was made possible by a Faculty Research Grant from the Social Science Research Council, and I wish to express my appreciation for the financial and other assistance given me by the North Carolina Business Foundation and the Institute for Research in Social Science. I wish also to acknowledge my indebtedness to the Alumni Annual Giving funds of the University of North Carolina administered by the University Research Council and to the Ford Foundation for a grant under its program for assisting American university presses in the publication of works in the humanities and the social sciences.

JAMES C. INGRAM

CONTENTS

TABLES

FIGURES

REGIONAL PAYMENTS MECHANISMS:
THE CASE OF PUERTO RICO

CHAPTER I

INTRODUCTION: ECONOMIC RELATIONS
BETWEEN PUERTO RICO AND THE
UNITED STATES

For the study of interregional economic adjustment
within the United States "common market" area, Puerto
Rico offers important advantages, some of which are
unique to her. The Puerto Rican economy is closely integrated with the United States economy, and no tariffs or
other restrictions are placed on trade between the two
economies. They use a common monetary unit whose
regulation and control are in the hands of national authorities; they share a common citizenship; and they share a
legal and judicial system founded on the United States
Constitution. This legal system guarantees property rights
and provides a common rule of law which greatly facilitates
the movement of capital.

Thus it seems clear that in spite of her geographical
separation Puerto Rico may be treated as a region of the
United States. Indeed, this separation becomes an advantage, for it partly accounts for our ability to measure
economic transactions between the two economies, and it
provides a clear-cut delineation of the regional boundaries.
In a field such as "regional science," where exact definition
is rarely possible, this clarity is a welcome relief.

Although Puerto Rico is part of the total United States
economy and may be treated as a region, it is also possible
to treat her as a nation and to make use of international
trade analogies. This possibility exists because of the

abundance of economic statistics—statistics that have been organized to treat Puerto Rico "as if" she were a nation. The availability of these economic statistics enables us to analyze the economic relationships between the United States and Puerto Rico, taken as a region of the total United States economy, more completely and in far greater detail than can be done for any continental state or region. The abundance of economic statistics in Puerto Rico is in part attributable to her unique political status as a quasi-autonomous Commonwealth "associated" with the United States.[1] For example, the United States Department of Commerce continues to collect statistics of United States trade with Puerto Rico and thereby provides a valuable source of data on the volume and composition of external trade of Puerto Rico. This collection ceased in 1948 for Alaska and Hawaii, a circumstance that greatly hampers the formulation of reliable balance-of-payments estimates for those states. While we will not enter the debate about Puerto Rico's political status, it can be said with confidence that either statehood or full independence would remove the peculiar advantages she possesses for the purpose of this study—statehood would dry up important sources of data, and independence would take Puerto Rico out of the United States economy and remove the regional analogy.[2]

In any case, the present study is possible only because of the existence of well-organized economic statistics for Puerto Rico. The Puerto Rican Planning Board developed comprehensive income and product accounts and balance-of-payments statistics during World War II. These statis-

1. The title Commonwealth of Puerto Rico is rendered in Spanish as Estado Libre Asociado de Puerto Rico.

2. In view of the heated nature of the debate about status, we should explicitly state that this passage is not intended as an argument for or against any of the three alternatives being considered. For an excellent discussion of the background of, and issues in, this debate, see Robert J. Hunter, *Puerto Rico, A Survey of Historical, Economic, and Political Affairs*, House Committee on Interior and Insular Affairs, 86th Cong., 1st Sess. (Washington: G.P.O., 1959).

tics have been standardized and published on a continuous basis ever since. In what follows we shall rely heavily on these and other economic statistics for the Puerto Rican economy.

For those interested in the study of a city, or metropolitan area, Puerto Rico might also be regarded a a city. To be sure, her geographical separation then becomes a disadvantage because it alters some of the economic relationships with the hinterland in comparison with those of the typical mainland city; but in area, population, and dependence upon the rest of the economy, Puerto Rico's position is analogous to that of a city. For example, Puerto Rico's area and population (3500 sq. mi.; 2,100,000) may be compared with those of large metropolitan areas in the United States, such as Los Angeles and Miami. Puerto Rico is considerably more compact, homogeneous, and densely populated than some of the "urban areas" now being studied in the United States, such as the "Piedmont crescent" in North Carolina or the massive Washington-Boston super-city.

Whether one wishes to regard Puerto Rico as a city, state, or region of the United States, our interest centers on the opportunity to apply international trade analogies to economic relations between Puerto Rico and the rest of the United States. The similarities of interregional and international trade and payments have long been recognized and accepted, but little actual study of the interregional case has been attempted.[3] Efforts to make such studies within the United States have been frustrated for lack of data. The result is that we have little precise knowledge about the process of regional interaction and adjustment within the United States.

In this study we shall study the economic relationships between Puerto Rico and the United States in two related frameworks. First, we shall seek to estimate the gross

3. For an excellent summary and analysis of efforts that have been made, see W. Isard *et al.*, *Methods of Regional Analysis* (New York: Technology Press and John Wiley, 1960), Chapter 5.

flows of funds to and from the Puerto Rican economy, using existing balance-of-payments data to break down the gross flows into their component parts. Such a breakdown cannot be accomplished for mainland interregional moneyflows, a fact which has hampered efforts to utilize Federal Reserve data on flows of funds through the Interdistrict Settlement Fund. Second, we shall apply conventional balance-of-payments theory to the Puerto Rican case, analyzing the impact of recent inflows of capital, the mechanism of adjustment in the balance of payments, and the interactions with income and prices.

The statement made above, that Puerto Rico lies within the United States tariff zone and that no restrictions exist on trade between the United States and Puerto Rico, requires some qualification. Puerto Rican exports do enter the United States market free of duty, and the only important restriction concerns quota limitations on shipments of sugar. As a matter of fact, because Puerto Rico does not meet her full sugar quota, this program does not now hamper her sugar exports. Indeed, she benefits from the higher United States price received for sugar exports. The sugar program controls the amounts of raw and refined sugar shipped from Puerto Rico, however, and the effect of this aspect has been to prevent the development of refinery capacity in Puerto Rico and thus to limit her to the role of a raw material supplier. Only about 12 per cent of Puerto Rican sugar exports to the United States may take the form of refined sugar at the present time.

The other side of this coin—Puerto Rican restrictions on imports from the United States (and elsewhere)—requires more discussion. By law, the Commonwealth government cannot impose tariffs on imports or exports, but it can impose excise taxes. When no domestic production exists, it is difficult to distinguish between an "excise tax" and an import duty.[4] Certainly the economic effect of the tax is not changed by labeling it an excise tax instead of an import duty, as long as domestic production does not begin.

Puerto Rico has imposed a sizable number of excise taxes, mostly on articles not produced within the island. These taxes have exactly the same economic effect as a tariff on United States goods entering Puerto Rico.[5] A summary of the principal excise taxes in force in 1959 is given below:[6]

Ad Valorem

Rugs	20%
Chewing gum and candies	15%
Knives, spoons, and forks (cost over $1.00/unit)	20%
Photographic equipment	15%
Jewelry articles	20%
Electrical or gas appliances	15%
Radios (cost over $50)	5%
Television sets (cost over $150)	15%
Passenger cars:	
Taxable price under $2,000	20%
Taxable price $2,000-2,500	$400 plus 60% of amount over $2,000
Taxable price over $2,500	$700 plus 80% of amount over $2,500

Specific

Cement, per 100 lbs.	$0.03

4. Lawyers tell me this is a cloudy issue in court cases, but I have not examined the technical legal questions.

5. Excise taxes are paid on designated articles regardless of place of origin. Imports from third countries pay the U.S. tariff in addition to the Puerto Rican excise tax.

6. *What You Should Know about Taxes in Puerto Rico*, Commonwealth of Puerto Rico, Department of the Treasury, San Juan, Puerto Rico, 1959.

Matches, per gross (25-50 in a box)	$0.15
Cinematographic films, per linear foot	$0.02
Tires, per pound	$0.08
Tubes, per pound	$0.09
Gasoline, per gallon	$0.08
Cigarettes, per package of 20	$0.21
Distilled spirits, per proof gallon	$6.00-$12.00
Beer, per wine gallon	$0.50-$0.60

While most states levy excise taxes for revenue purposes on such products as tobacco and distilled liquor, the use of these taxes by Puerto Rico has gone much further. The primary purpose of the taxes is probably still to raise revenue, but other purposes also play a role. For example, the steeply graduated tax on automobiles is probably intended to reduce the number of automobiles in use and thus to alleviate pressure on the highway system. Higher rates on more expensive cars are expected to reduce traffic and parking problems, as well as to reduce the amount of income spent for imports. The tax also has redistributive intent, as a progressive tax on luxury consumption.[7]

These excise taxes may not have had much influence on the total value of imports, but they have probably altered the composition of imports a good deal. About half of Commonwealth *tax* revenues come from such taxes, but it may be that the government spends about the same proportion for imports as the taxpayer would have spent.

7. To illustrate this point, consider the effective rate of tax on a small car selling in New York for $1500 compared to a larger car selling there for $4000. The small car would pay a 20 per cent tax in Puerto Rico and would sell there for under $2000, including tax. The larger car would pay $2100 in tax, or the equivalent of 52 per cent ad valorem, and would sell for $6100 in Puerto Rico.

CHAPTER II

FLOWS OF FUNDS TO AND FROM PUERTO RICO

Our purpose in this part of the study is to measure the gross flows of money to and from Puerto Rico. That is, we seek to measure the total amount of money payments made to the rest of the world by all Puerto Rican residents, regardless of the form in which the money payment is made or its purpose. Similarly, we seek to measure the total money receipts of Puerto Rican residents from the rest of the world. Such a measure of moneyflows is related to the balance of payments, but it is much "grosser" than the balance of payments as usually presented. That is, the moneyflows sum includes a great many transactions that are netted out in the balance of payments, particularly in the capital account. However, we will later use balance-of-payments estimates to separate at least the major components of moneyflows.

Most Puerto Rican money payments to, and receipts from, the rest of the world are made through Puerto Rican commercial banks—such payments and receipts are made by checks and drafts which are settled through correspondent accounts maintained in external banks by Puerto Rican banks.

In this study, we use the term "Puerto Rican commercial banks" to include all commercial banks operating in Puerto Rico, whether locally chartered or not. During most of the period we cover, there were eleven commercial banks in Puerto Rico. Of these eleven banks, seven were chartered by the Commonwealth, two were branches of New York banks, and two were branches of Canadian banks. When we speak of "correspondent accounts," we include the home-office accounts of the New York and Canadian branches as well as the accounts of Commonwealth-chartered banks with their New York correspondents.

In 1960 the author spent several months in Puerto Rico, during which time all Puerto Rican banks were requested to supply figures showing total debits and credits in their correspondent accounts. These figures, which the banks generously supplied, constitute the major part of the total flow of funds to and from the island.

A detailed description of transactions through the banking system, and of the various forms these transactions may take, is given in an appendix to this chapter on page 28. This appendix also contains a statement of the accounting method underlying our moneyflows estimates. Here we wish to take note of the fact that not all money payments to and from the island go through Puerto Rican commercial banks.

Some transactions are made through accounts held in external banks by Puerto Rican firms, individuals, or government agencies. For example, when a Puerto Rican firm maintains a checking account in a New York bank, it may make payments to mainland suppliers by drawing checks against this external account, and it may deposit the proceeds of export sales to this account. Such transactions do not appear in the records of Puerto Rican commercial banks, but they should be treated as transactions between the Puerto Rican economy and the rest of the world, and they should be included in our estimates. Information about this class of transactions proved difficult to acquire, however, and in the end we obtained such information only for Puerto Rican government agencies (including public authorities). There is reason to believe that the volume of transactions of this type by the private sector is not more than 3 per cent of the total moneyflows, and it may be even less. This estimate is especially applicable to the period after 1957, for the exchange charge levied by Puerto Rican banks on mainland clearings was removed in that year. This matter will be further discussed in the appendix to this chapter.

Other means of payment that may not be reflected in the records of Puerto Rican commercial banks are the following:

1. Currency movements.
2. Money orders.
3. Intra-firm accounting transfers, *e.g.*, between a Puerto Rican branch and its mainland home office.

Currency

Coin and currency taken in and out of Puerto Rico by travelers cannot be directly measured. Currency requirements of banks and the business community are supplied through a special Custody Account of the United States Treasury Department which is maintained in a local commercial bank, the San Juan branch of the First National City Bank of New York. Information about currency movements through this account was obtained. Somewhat to our surprise, the Custody Account figures show a net *export* of currency from Puerto Rico in recent years. However, we have assumed, as does the Planning Board, that *net* movements of currency were zero or, in other words, that currency brought in by travelers offsets the net outflow that appears in the Custody Account. In any case the amounts are so small in relation to gross flows of funds that they can be omitted without harm.

Money Orders

Estimates of transactions made through postal money orders are available. These estimates are made by the Balance of Payments Section of the Planning Board. The amounts are very small in relation to gross flows of funds.

Intra-firm Transfers

Somewhat different problems are raised in the case of transfers made by accounting entries to reflect charges and credits between a branch and its home office. Are these moneyflows? Technically they are not, but it can be argued that moneyflows should be imputed in the case of such transactions. We have elected to exclude these intra-firm transactions from our moneyflows estimates. This choice is made in part because of the extreme difficulty of obtaining accurate information about intra-firm transfers. There is some evidence that the volume of transactions of this type is not great, however. Many of the newly established branches and subsidiaries of mainland firms have been careful to use explicit money payments (usually employing separate bank accounts in local banks) in order to safeguard their rights to tax exemption.

Broadly speaking, we define the "economy of Puerto Rico" to include all persons, firms, government agencies, and other organizations that are "residents" of Puerto Rico. This definition is further discussed in the section on method, below, but a comment on the treatment of the federal government is required at this point. We shall treat the federal government as part of the rest of the world, and all its transactions with the Puerto Rican private and public sectors are counted as part of Puerto Rican transactions with the external world, even when the federal agency is physically located in Puerto Rico. The great bulk of federal payments to, and receipts from, Puerto Rico are accomplished through debits and credits to the Treasurer's General Accounts which are maintained by the United States Treasury Department in certain Puerto Rican commercial banks.

We have compiled moneyflows estimates for three fiscal years: 1957-58, 1958-59, and 1959-60. The choice of these years was dictated partly by availability of data and partly by the fact, already mentioned above, that the exchange charge formerly levied by Puerto Rican banks on mainland clearings was removed in 1957. Removal of this charge led to the transfer of many accounts from mainland to insular banks, and therefore a larger part of total money-flows now goes through Puerto Rican banks than was the case before 1957.

For regions within the continental United States, the closest analogy to our moneyflows measures is found in the flows of funds among Federal Reserve districts, as reported by the Federal Reserve Interdistrict Settlement Fund. These flows are not as comprehensive as our Puerto Rican estimates, however, because IDSF data omit check clearings that go directly through correspondent banks, some movements of currency, money orders, and certain other monetary transfers, as well as intra-firm transfers. Some of these are also omitted from our estimates, but it seems likely that omissions from our estimates are relatively smaller than from IDSF data.

Another disadvantage of IDSF data is that the gross flows cannot be classified by type of transaction or by transactor. The conference held by the Board of Governors in 1955 was dominated by this problem, and a note of frustration runs through the entire conference report.[1] Indeed, it appears that the inability to separate commercial and financial components of IDSF flows has proved to be a rock on which interregional moneyflows research has foundered in the United States. Some such separation seems to be essential if the data are to be useful for economic analysis; the gross, unclassified flows have failed to yield much economic signifiance.

It is partly because of the deficiencies of mainland data that we are interested in the flows of funds to and from Puerto Rico. These are also "interregional moneyflows," but the existence of reliable balance-of-payments estimates will permit some classification of the gross flows. It will also be possible to classify by type of transactor or at least

1. *Record of the Federal Reserve System Conference on the Interregional Flow of Funds*, Washington, D.C., April 1955, mimeographed.

to separate governmental and private sectors in each of our two "regions."

Our moneyflows estimates are summarized in Table 1. The three sections of this table contain gross money payments from Puerto Rico to the rest of the world (RoW), gross money receipts from the rest of the world, and the net inflows or outflows.

It can be seen that gross moneyflows to and from Puerto Rico have risen sharply from 1958 to 1960. Thus total payments to RoW rose from $2,510 million in 1958 to $3,102 million in 1959 and to $4,033 million in 1960. Receipts were approximately the same. For 1960, total external moneyflows were more than twice the value of gross insular product and over three times the value of gross imports (current account debits in the balance of payments). These ratios imply a sizable volume of activity in short-term capital over and above the financing involved in the trade in goods and services. These relationships also indicate the enormous importance of external transactions to the Puerto Rican economy. Further evidence of this importance is given by the fact that total payments to RoW have been equal to about one-half of total debits to bank accounts in Puerto Rico in these three years. While the use of currency is relatively larger in Puerto Rico than in the United States, this fact nevertheless indicates the extent to which Puerto Rico is integrated into the world (especially the United States mainland) payments system.

In Table 1 the Puerto Rican economy and the rest of the world are each divided into two sectors, one private and one governmental, and receipts and payments are shown between each domestic sector and each RoW sector. The RoW sectors are "federal government" and "other RoW." The latter includes transactions with governments other than the United States, but such transactions are extremely small in amount.

Table 1

Flow of Funds between Puerto Rico and the Rest of the World[a]

(millions of dollars)

A. Payments from Puerto Rico to RoW

Fiscal Year	FROM PR PRIVATE SECTOR		FROM PR GOVERNMENT		FROM PR TOTAL ECONOMY	
	To Fed. Govt. (I)	To RoW Pvt. Sect. (G+H)	To Fed. Govt. (J)	To RoW Pvt. Sect. (K+L)	To Fed. Govt. (I+J)	To RoW Pvt. Sect. (G+H+ K+L)
1958	−289	−2027	−10	−184	−299	−2211
1959	−319	−2581	− 8	−194	−327	−2775
1960	−375	−3421	−11	−226	−386	−3647

B. Receipts of Puerto Rico from RoW

Fiscal Year	BY PR PRIVATE SECTOR		BY PR GOVERNMENT		BY PR TOTAL ECONOMY	
	From Fed. Govt. (C)	From RoW Pvt. Sect. (A+B)	From Fed. Govt. (D)	From RoW Pvt. Sect. (E+F)	From Fed. Govt. (C+D)	From RoW Pvt. Sect. (A+B+ E+F)
1958	441	1789	72	211	513	2000
1959	475	2391	59	224	534	2615
1960	515	3231	61	245	576	3476

C. Net Flows

Fiscal Year	PR PRIVATE SECTOR		PR GOVERNMENT		PR TOTAL ECONOMY	
	Fed. Govt.	RoW Pvt. Sect.	Fed. Govt.	RoW Pvt. Sect.	Fed. Govt.	RoW Pvt. Sect.
1958	+152	− 238	+62	+ 27	+214	− 211
1959	+156	− 190	+51	+ 30	+207	− 160
1960	+140	− 190	+50	+ 19	+190	− 171

[a] Letters in column headings refer to transaction types defined in the Appendix to Chapter II.

SOURCES: Figures in this table were compiled from data made available to the author by Puerto Rican banks, the Commonwealth Treasury and Public Authorities, and the United States Treasury Department. Sources are described in the text of Chapter II and its Appendix.

We observe that receipts from the federal government exceeded payments to the federal government for both the Puerto Rican government and the Puerto Rican private sector. In the case of the Puerto Rican government, receipts from the federal government arise primarily from federal donations for public health, roads, education, and similar programs, and from refunds of federal excise and customs taxes to the Commonwealth government; the most important payment to the federal government is for social security taxes for employees of the Commonwealth government.[2]

The flows of funds between Puerto Rico and the federal government are summarized in Table 2, which is taken

Table 2

Transactions with Federal Government

(millions of dollars)

	Year	Puerto Rican Private Sector	Puerto Rican Government	Total
Payments to	1958	−289	−10	−299
Fed. Govt.	1959	−319	− 8	−327
	1960	−375	−11	−386
Receipts from	1958	+441	+72	+513
Fed. Govt.	1959	+475	+59	+534
	1960	+515	+61	+576
Net Receipts	1958	+152	+62	+214
	1959	+156	+51	+207
	1960	+140	+50	+190

2. As will be further explained below, Commonwealth government transactions in U.S. securities are not treated as transactions with the federal government. The reason is that such transactions are, for the most part, carried on in the New York money market, and when the Commonwealth government buys such bonds it is usually dealing with a private firm in New York. Nor do these transactions appear in the U.S. Treasurer's General Accounts in Puerto Rican banks.

from Table 1. It can be seen that both of the Puerto Rican sectors (private and governmental) have a net receipt of funds from the federal government.

Receipts of the Puerto Rican private sector from the federal government include federal transfer payments to individuals and a large part of the operational disbursements of federal agencies in Puerto Rico. The gross volume of private sector transactions with the federal government is inflated by sales and redemptions of United States savings bonds. These transactions appear in the above figures because they are handled through the Treasurer's General Accounts and not through the private financial market. Thus they are transactions between the federal government and the Puerto Rican private sector.

Puerto Rican government receipts from the RoW private sector also exceeded payments to that sector, indicating that the Puerto Rican government is a net receiver of funds from RoW. These net receipts were primarily the result of the sale of Commonwealth securities (including both government and public authorities) in mainland financial markets. Indeed, the bulk of the gross transactions of Puerto Rican government with the RoW private sector is accounted for in the purchase and sale of securities. The turnover is as large as it is because of the turnover in short-term securities held by the Commonwealth government and because of activity in connection with new issues and sinking-fund investment accounts managed by mainland trustees. For example, when the Puerto Rican Water Resources Authority needs additional funds it may first borrow on a short-term basis from the First National City Bank of New York, its mainland trustee. When such temporary borrowing reaches (say) $15 million, a bond issue of $30 million may be floated. From the proceeds of this issue the temporary loan is paid off and the excess funds invested in short-term securities until needed. As construction bills come in they are paid with proceeds from the sale of these short-term securities.

Such a sequence generates a large volume of transactions between the Water Resources Authority and the RoW private sector. The trustee also manages sinking funds accumulated on outstanding bond issues, and the turnover in the securities held in these funds reaches sizable amounts.

The *net* receipts of the Puerto Rican government from the RoW private sector are no larger than they are because the Puerto Rican government is itself accumulating mainland securities in the investment portfolios that it maintains. These securities form the liquid reserves of the Commonwealth government, the assets of its pension funds, etc. Table 3 summarizes transactions between the two Puerto Rican sectors and the RoW private sector.

Table 3

Transactions with RoW Private Sector

(millions of dollars)

	Year	Puerto Rican Private Sector	Puerto Rican Government	Total
Payments to RoW	1958	$ −2027	$ −184	$ −2211
Private Sector	1959	−2581	−194	−2775
	1960	−3421	−226	−3647
Receipts from RoW	1958	+1789	+211	+2000
Private Sector	1959	+2391	+224	+2615
	1960	+3231	+245	+3476
Net Receipts (+)	1958	− 238	+ 27	− 211
Payments (−)	1959	− 190	+ 30	− 160
	1960	− 190	+ 19	− 171

INVERSE RELATION BETWEEN FEDERAL AND PRIVATE FLOWS

It can be seen in Tables 2 and 3 that the net receipts from the federal government by the Puerto Rican private sector (plus the smaller net receipts from the RoW private sector by the Puerto Rican government) are roughly matched by net payments to the RoW private sector by the Puerto Rican private sector. This inverse relation is substantially equivalent to the familiar inverse relation between federal transfers and commercial and financial transactions, which has been observed in regional money-flows on the United States mainland. In each of the three years for which we have figures, Puerto Rican receipts from the federal government exceeded Puerto Rican payments to the federal government, and this excess of receipts is matched by an excess of outpayments in "all other" transactions. The figures (in millions) are as follows:

Year	Puerto Rican Net Receipts from Federal Government	Puerto Rican Net Payments to RoW Private Sector
1958	$ +214	$ −211
1959	+207	−160
1960	+190	−171

It seems clear that this inverse relationship is systematic, not accidental. (The relationship also holds in all except three months of the three-year period for which we have data. See Table 5, below). This is indeed a definitional relationship analogous to the necessary equality between current account and capital account balances (with opposite signs) in the balance of payments. Except for changes in reserve balances, total receipts of the Puerto Rican economy must equal total payments made to RoW. Total receipts and payments are each classified into transactions with the federal government and with RoW private sector (all other). If there is a net receipt (inflow) of funds from the federal government in any accounting period, then by definition there must be a net payment (outflow) of funds to the RoW private sector. This results because the two classifications exhaust the total receipts and payments, and their net balances must be equal and opposite in sign (except for changes in reserves). While this is a simple point, it has not been clearly understood.[3] An example will help to illustrate the argument. Suppose total receipts and payments in a given period amount to $100, and receipts and payments from the federal government are known to be $40.00 and $15.00, respectively. We then have the following:

	Payments	Receipts	Net
Federal Government	$ 15	$ 40	$ +25
RoW Private Sector	?	?	?
Total	$100	$100	$ 0

Now it is obvious that the missing transactions with RoW private sector can be filled in at once. Payments are $85.00, receipts $60.00, and the net payment is $−25.00, exactly offsetting the net receipts from federal government.

Beyond the accounting aspects of this inverse relation, one may ask which is the autonomous element and which the induced. Considering the nature of federal programs involving payments to Puerto Rico, it seems likely that these are autonomously determined and that the necessary adaptations to the treasury flows are made in the commercial and financial transactions of other sectors. Federal payments to Puerto Rican firms and individuals (or to the government) permit the recipients to buy more goods and services or to hold more financial assets than they otherwise could. No matter which choice they make, the result is that payments from the Puerto Rican economy (including the banking sector) to non-federal external sectors will be higher than they would otherwise be. If payments to and receipts from the RoW private sector by the Puerto Rican economy were formerly equal, payments will now exceed receipts.

3. Hobart Carr and Douglas Hellweg appear to have had a similar definitional relation in mind in their comments about the inverse relation between treasury transfers and commercial and financial transactions that has been observed in Interdistrict Settlement Fund data. *Record of the Federal Reserve System Conference on the Interregional Flow of Funds.*

The autonomous nature of the federal transfers can be shown by considering the effect of a change in each of the flows. An increase in federal expenditures in Puerto Rico would not be accompanied by much of an increase in payments to the federal government, and the net inflow of United States Treasury funds would rise. This inflow would be matched by a rise in commercial and financial payments to other sectors in RoW, whether for the purchase of goods and services or for acquisition of assets. Individuals and firms receiving payments from the federal government will tend to increase their expenditures, some of which will be made for imports. To the extent that the additional funds are not spent for imports of goods and services, banks will be left with additional external balances, and they will be likely to use these to buy securities in RoW financial markets. In either case, the inflow of federal funds gives rise to an equal offsetting outflow. A decrease in defense expenditures would similarly induce an equilibrating (accommodating) response in commercial and financial flows.

On the other hand, an increase in commercial payments to RoW would not induce much change in United States Treasury transfers. Instead, an increase in imports (payments to RoW) would in the first instance be matched by the sale of commercial bank assets (an increase in receipts from RoW), both of which would be included in commercial and financial transactions. Forces may be set in motion to reduce this volume of receipts and payments, but they are not likely to produce or evoke responses in the volume or net balance of treasury transfers.

This conclusion—that in the determination of the size and direction of the net balance between federal transfers and commercial and financial transactions, it is the federal flows which are autonomous—may not apply to inter-regional payments in the United States mainland, but it seems likely that it does. Casual inspection of federal expenditures and transfer payments suggests that the great bulk of federal outlays are not undertaken in response to the payments positions of the several regions. Even those federal programs with a specific redistributive intent are not varied in response to regional payments pressures. Similarly, federal revenues do not, for the most part, vary in such a way as to produce an equilibrating response to regional payments pressures.

While the bulk of federal outlays and receipts appear to be autonomously determined, at least as far as short-run disturbances in regional balances of payments are concerned, it can nevertheless be seen that *some* federal operations do play an accommodating role. We shall mention only a few examples. On the expenditures side, the federal government attempts, when feasible, to award contracts for construction or procurement in so-called depressed areas of the country. To the extent that expenditures are actually increased in these areas, an inflow of federal funds arises, an inflow that will tend to relieve the payments pressures resulting from an economic disturbance. Purchases and sales of mortgages by the Federal National Mortgage Association (FNMA) may also play a modest equilibrating role.[4] In a region with payments pressures, interest rates will tend to rise, credit will be less available, and local financial institutions may sell mortgages on a larger scale to the FNMA. Since the FNMA may then sell the mortgages to institutions in other regions, its net effect is to induce a flow of private funds from one region to another. However, with respect to the first region, the provision of funds by the FNMA may be regarded as an accommodating response. On the revenue side, it is clear that federal income and excise taxes will decline in a depressed area and, even if expenditures are unchanged, an equilibrating response in net federal flows of funds is indicated.

The above remarks are intended merely as illustrations

4. See Saul B. Klaman, *The Postwar Residential Mortgage Market* (Princeton: Princeton University Press, 1961), especially pp. 95-98, 226-27.

of the problem. The regional effect of federal outlays and receipts is a subject that needs to be studied, and we are in no position to reach firm conclusions. With respect to Puerto Rico, however, it can be said that federal flows are largely autonomous since most of the examples of equilibrating responses do not apply to Puerto Rico.

SEPARATION OF COMMERICAL AND FINANCIAL COMPONENTS

By using data from the Puerto Rican balance of payments estimates, we are able to break down our gross moneyflows totals into their commercial and financial components. Such a separation is possible because some items in the balance of payments are already reported on a *gross* basis. This is true of the current account items (merchandise, services, investment income), unilateral transfers (both private and governmental), and some of the long-term capital categories. The principal items in the balance of payments that are shown on a net basis are the various short-term capital categories, and two long-term capital items: "external investments in mortgages and other loans" and "Puerto Rican long-term assets abroad." Direct investment is also shown on a net basis, but the gross amounts would not differ much from the net figures available.

We can therefore list all payments and receipts that are available on a gross basis in the balance of payments and then, using our gross moneyflows totals, we can calculate the residual, which will be primarily short-term capital. This computation is shown in Table 4. There it can be seen that the "commercial component"—*i.e.* the transactions involving purchase and sale of goods and services—declined from 38 to 29 per cent of the total flows on the payments side, and from 27 to 22 per cent of total flows on the receipts side. The actual percentages, for visible trade and for total goods and services, are as follows:

Percentage of Total Moneyflows Accounted For By

Fiscal Year	Payments to RoW		Receipts from RoW	
	Visible Trade	All Goods and Services	Visible Trade	All Goods and Services
1958	30%	38%	19%	27%
1959	27%	34%	17%	24%
1960	23%	29%	16%	22%

Table 4

Gross Flows of Funds and Balance-of-Payments Components

(millions of dollars)

	1958	1959	1960
Payments to RoW			
Current Account	$ 962	$1058	$1186
Unilateral Transfers	49	47	47
Long-term Capital	29	35	51
Short-term Capital[a]	1470	1962	2749
Total	$2510	$3102	$4033
Receipts from RoW			
Current Account	$ 681	$ 744	$ 882
Unilateral Transfers	173	175	169
Long-term Capital	220	190	202
Short-term Capital[a]	1439	2040	2799
Total	$2513	$3149	$4052

[a] Figures for short-term capital are calculated as a residual, using total flows of funds from Table 1.
SOURCES: Table 1, above, and *Balance of Payments, Puerto Rico, 1959*, Commonwealth of Puerto Rico, Planning Board. 1960 figures supplied by Balance-of-Payments Section, Planning Board.

The relative shares of commercial transactions in total moneyflows have thus declined in these three years, for both payments and receipts.

It should be emphasized that the gross estimates derived for short-term capital in Table 4 do not include intra-firm transactions which do not involve actual payments. Our gross totals represent estimates of actual

Table 5
Flow of Funds between Puerto Rico and the Rest of World by Months, July, 1957, to June, 1960

(millions of dollars)

Year and Month	PAYMENTS FROM PUERTO RICO		RECEIPTS OF PUERTO RICO		NET FLOWS (+ Receipts, − Payments)	
	To Fed. Govt.	To RoW Pvt. Sect.	From Fed. Govt.	From RoW Pvt. Sect.	Fed. Govt.	RoW Pvt. Sect.
1957						
July	18.7	149.5	38.2	123.7	+19.5	−25.8
Aug.	25.2	149.0	40.9	134.8	+15.7	−14.2
Sept.	19.6	145.9	42.7	122.4	+23.1	−23.5
Oct.	29.5	154.8	55.5	130.8	+26.0	−24.0
Nov.	25.1	152.2	45.7	131.8	+20.6	−20.4
Dec.	28.9	183.5	40.9	176.6	+12.0	− 6.9
1958						
Jan.	21.8	198.9	48.4	175.9	+26.6	−23.0
Feb.	24.2	146.4	40.3	150.6	+16.1	+ 4.2
Mar.	28.0	206.9	39.4	186.4	+11.4	−20.5
Apr.	25.2	183.0	39.3	169.5	+14.1	−13.5
May	27.5	216.6	40.1	185.7	+12.6	−30.9
Jun.	24.3	235.8	41.8	224.0	+17.5	−11.8
July	25.4	191.3	48.1	174.5	+22.7	−16.8
Aug.	24.9	183.4	40.5	175.4	+15.6	− 8.0
Sept.	24.3	192.1	43.0	178.4	+18.7	−13.7
Oct.	26.6	198.1	44.4	179.6	+17.8	−18.5
Nov.	24.0	187.9	47.4	164.4	+23.4	−23.5
Dec.	30.2	275.1	46.6	252.2	+16.4	−22.9
1959						
Jan.	21.1	191.0	47.1	166.3	+26.0	−24.7
Feb.	30.9	198.3	37.9	188.8	+ 7.0	− 9.5
Mar.	27.1	279.3	42.5	257.3	+15.4	−22.0
Apr.	30.9	234.7	49.2	216.0	+18.3	−18.7
May	33.1	249.3	43.0	285.6	+ 9.9	+36.3
Jun.	28.4	302.8	44.9	283.4	+16.5	−19.4
July	33.5	281.1	47.8	266.3	+14.3	−14.8
Aug.	30.5	255.1	47.6	239.5	+16.1	−15.6
Sept.	25.9	268.5	43.7	232.2	+17.8	−36.3
Oct.	27.6	255.4	53.0	239.5	+25.4	−15.9
Nov.	43.5	308.0	48.2	304.6	+ 4.7	− 3.4
Dec.	43.9	305.0	49.4	296.1	+ 5.5	− 8.9

(Table 5 continued)

(millions of dollars)

| Year and Month | PAYMENTS FROM PUERTO RICO | | RECEIPTS OF PUERTO RICO | | NET FLOWS (+ Receipts, − Payments) | |
	To Fed. Govt.	To RoW Pvt. Sect.	From Fed. Govt.	From RoW Pvt. Sect.	Fed. Govt.	RoW Pvt. Sect.
1960						
Jan.	24.9	293.4	48.6	251.4	+23.7	−42.0
Feb.	32.9	280.4	45.9	262.4	+13.0	−18.0
Mar.	30.2	315.0	49.7	302.2	+19.5	−12.8
Apr.	30.6	303.8	46.3	298.3	+15.7	− 5.5
May	34.0	301.9	48.8	304.1	+14.8	+ 2.2
Jun.	28.8	368.2	46.8	367.7	+18.0	− 0.5

SOURCES. Figures in this table were compiled from data made available to the author by Puerto Rican banks, the Commonwealth Treasury and Public Authorities, and the United States Treasury Department. Sources are described in Chapter II and its Appendix.

money payments; we have not included imputed items. Since some portion of commercial transactions in goods and services, as well as the long-term capital items, do not actually involve money payments, our treatment somewhat understates the magnitude of short-term capital relative to the total flows. Or, conversely, it exaggerates the importance of commercial transactions because some purchases and sales of goods and services do not in fact give rise to moneyflows. We think such exaggeration is small, however.

We also obtained estimates of moneyflows to and from Puerto Rico on a monthly basis from July, 1957, to June, 1960. These estimates are presented in Table 5. The monthly figures are less complete than those given above for fiscal years; specifically, monthly figures do not include transactions of government and the public authorities made through deposits held directly in United States banks, nor do they include money orders and currency movements. The monthly figures thus refer primarily to transactions made through clearing accounts of Puerto Rican banks and the Treasurer's General Accounts in the insular banks.

The inverse relation between federal and private flows of funds holds for all except three of the thirty-six months in these three years.

APPENDIX TO CHAPTER II

DEFINITIONS AND METHODS

Broadly speaking, we define the "economy of Puerto Rico" to include all persons, firms, government agencies, and other organizations which are "residents" of Puerto Rico, except agencies of the federal government. Mainlanders employed by firms in Puerto Rico are residents of Puerto Rico and are treated as part of the Puerto Rican economy. Branches and subsidiaries of United States firms are considered as residents of Puerto Rico, and their transactions are therefore included in our moneyflows estimates except where intra-firm accounting transfers are used. Puerto Ricans living in New York and elsewhere on the mainland are not considered to be part of the economy of Puerto Rico. Their remittances to relatives in Puerto Rico are treated as receipts from the external world. The United States government is treated as a non-resident, including even the United States agencies and installations physically located in Puerto Rico. Treatment of the federal government is a troublesome matter, but to treat it as part of the external economy seems vastly preferable to any alternative treatment. By and large, our definition of the economy of Puerto Rico corresponds to the definition used by the balance-of-payments section of the Planning Board.

To make clear the nature of the empirical problem and to explain how the estimates are derived, we shall describe some pertinent features of the institutional structure of the Puerto Rican economy.

The great bulk of Puerto Rico's external transactions are with the United States and they are denominated in dollars. The chief problem, therefore, is to measure the flow of money payments to and from the United States. Since most of these payments are made through bank transfers, we shall want to obtain the total value of such clearings between the two economies. Actually, we are interested in gross flows of funds between Puerto Rico and the rest of the world, and this is what we shall try to measure, but in the following discussion we often speak only of transactions with the United States.

Check clearings with the United States mainland do not take place through the Federal Reserve banks, for the most part. Puerto Rico is a part of the United States monetary system, but it is not formally a part of the Federal Reserve System, and Puerto Rican banks are not member-banks in that system.[5] The great bulk of the checks cleared between Puerto Rico and the mainland are settled through the correspondent accounts of Puerto Rican banks with mainland banks. The most important of these accounts are in New York commercial banks. Mainland banks also maintain accounts with Puerto Rican banks, and some transactions are settled through these accounts.

Commercial banking services in Puerto Rico are provided by eleven banks, several of which have branches scattered around the island. These eleven banks include seven Commonwealth-chartered banks, two branches of New York commercial banks (one national bank, one state-chartered), and two branches of Canadian commercial banks. The complete list follows, with total assets added to furnish an indication of relative size and importance.

Commercial Banks in Puerto Rico[6] as of Dec. 31, 1959
(millions of dollars)

Bank	*Total Assets*
Commonwealth chartered:	
Banco de Popular	$148
Banco Crédito y Ahorro	114
Banco de Ponce	71
Banco de San Juan	15

5. Two New York member banks have branches in Puerto Rico, however, and one Puerto Rican bank maintains a non-member clearing account with the Federal Reserve Bank of New York.

6. Supplied by Bureau of Bank Examinations, Department of the Treasury, Commonwealth of Puerto Rico.

Roig Commercial Bank	7
Banco de San Germán	3
Banco de Economía y Préstamos	4
United States branches:	
First National City Bank of New York	126
Chase Manhattan Bank	83
Canadian branches:	
Royal Bank of Canada	20
Bank of Nova Scotia	17
Total	$608

In the "normal" case, payments to mainland firms and individuals are made by checks drawn on Puerto Rican banks and deposited in mainland banks, and receipts of Puerto Rican firms and individuals from mainland sources are made by checks drawn on mainland banks and deposited in Puerto Rican banks. All such checks appear in the clearings of Puerto Rican banks with mainland banks, and the amounts involved can be obtained from the records of the eleven Puerto Rican banks.

Many other "payments circuits" also exist, however, and some of them do not involve the Puerto Rican commercial banks. A fuller description of various payments circuits will be given below.

As already noted above, we will treat the federal government as part of the "rest of the world" in this study. Since Puerto Rico is not part of a Federal Reserve district, the United States Treasury Department has made special arrangements with Puerto Rican banks to handle treasury business. It has designated four banks on the island as "general depositories." Each of these banks carries a Treasurer's General Account to which deposits of taxes, proceeds of debt sales, and other federal revenues may be made, and against which are charged treasury checks, maturing federal obligations,[7] and other legitimate debits.

7. However, bank transactions in U.S. government securities for their own account are handled through correspondents and do not appear in debits and

For our purposes, credits to the Treasurer's General Accounts are considered to be payments from Puerto Rico to the external world, while debits are considered receipts from the external world. Since charges to the Treasurer's General Accounts usually exceed local revenues, deposits of outside funds (called "restorations") are occasionally required to replenish the accounts. The United States Treasury Department has provided information about the volume of transactions in these accounts.[8]

In addition to Treasurer's General Accounts, Treasury Tax and Loan Accounts are maintained in several Puerto Rican banks. These accounts are managed in the same way as in mainland banks. Tax revenues and the proceeds of debt sales are deposited to the accounts, but no charges are made to them except for transfers to the Federal Reserve banks. Calls on the Tax and Loan Accounts are handled by the Federal Reserve Bank of New York, and Puerto Rican banks make payment by charging correspondent balances in the New York commercial banks. We treat credits to the Tax and Loan Accounts as payments to the external world. Because most federal taxes do not apply in Puerto Rico, transactions in these accounts are small. The Federal Reserve Bank of New York has provided information about the amounts of money transferred through calls on the Tax and Loan Accounts.

Currency flows present a problem, but such flows are presumed to be relatively small. No figures are available except for transactions in the Custody Account of the United States Treasury with the San Juan branch of the First National City Bank of New York. This account was established to provide a convenient supply of currency for the Puerto Rican economy. In effect, the custodian bank holds part of the treasury's cash balance. It is authorized to issue currency from this treasury cash, at the same time

credits to Treasurer's General Accounts. The same is true of transactions in such securities by the Commonwealth government and its agencies.

8. I wish to express my appreciation to W. T. Heffelfinger and H. A. Rabon of the U.S. Treasury Department for their kind assistance and cooperation.

crediting the Treasurer's General Accounts. Similarly, redundant (or worn-out) currency may be withdrawn from circulation by charging the Treasurer's General Accounts and adding the currency to Treasury cash. Puerto Rican banks use this custody account to adjust their own cash holdings. Except for the amounts taken in and out by travelers and private firms, all currency movements are channeled through this account.

Money payments can also be made by postal money orders. Estimates of money orders received from and sent to external residents are available from surveys made by the balance-of-payments section of the Puerto Rican Planning Board.

Transactions of the Commonwealth government with the external world are separately classified. Public authorities and municipalities are treated as part of the Commonwealth government in this study. The Commonwealth government keeps its funds in Puerto Rican banks, and its transactions with the external world therefore appear in the external clearings of these banks. Some of the public authorities maintain accounts in United States banks, however, and activity in these accounts must be obtained separately. Municipalities have few transactions with RoW, except for the sale and amortization of bonds.

The only sectoring we attempt to perform, then, is the division of the Puerto Rican economy into a Commonwealth government sector and a private (all other) sector, and division of the external economy into a United States government sector and a private (all other) sector. Thus our objective is to complete the following matrix table for each of the years chosen: 1958, 1959, 1960. (See next page.)

Even this modest degree of sectoring proved to be difficult, and there is danger of misinterpretation. Consider, for example, external payments made by the Commonwealth government. In the accounting system of the Commonwealth Treasury, payments made to private firms and individuals outside Puerto Rico can be identified.

From: Receipts of:	Federal Govt.	Other External	Total
Commonwealth Govt.			
P.R. Private Sector			
Total P.R. Economy			

To: Payments of:			
Commonwealth Govt.			
P.R. Private Sector			
Total P.R. Economy			

But such payments do not represent the total amount spent by the Commonwealth government for goods and services provided by the external private sector. Far from it. When the Commonwealth government purchases United States-made equipment, it will in most cases buy it from a local manufacturer's agent or distributor. The treasury payment is made to this local firm or person, and it will not be included in payments to the external private sector. In other words, this table reflects the money transactions, not the ultimate origin of the goods and services.

A similar problem arises in financial transactions with the federal government. When banks or private individuals buy United States securities, they commonly buy outstanding issues in the New York money market. The transaction involves a payment from the Puerto Rican private sector to the United States private sector, even though the security purchased is a United States government bond. It is difficult to make a clear distinction between private-to-government and private-to-private transactions, either conceptually or empirically, in such cases. We have consistently tried to use a transactor approach in the figures presented in Chapter II.

The moneyflows data we seek are not collected by any agency of government, and it is therefore necessary to obtain information from basic sources in order to build up the estimates. To collect information from government, the banking system, and private firms, we must have an over-all accounting framework in which to organize and interpret the data. The purpose of this section is to outline such a framework.

We begin by showing the typical forms of transactions between Puerto Rican residents and the external world. We will develop a simple accounting system to portray transactions of Puerto Rican firms and government with United States firms and government. The way these transactions appear in the records of Puerto Rican banks (if at all) will be specified so that the actual figures supplied by the banks can be properly interpreted. Because we are interested in moneyflows, we will focus on the money balances of Puerto Rican transactors (private and governmental), United States transactors, and the links between these two furnished by Puerto Rican and United States banks.

A condensed picture of the accounting structure is given in Table 6. For Puerto Rico, the non-bank transactors are divided into private and governmental sectors. For each of these sectors, a "T-account" is shown, representing that sector's demand deposit with Puerto Rican banks and with United States banks. For the Puerto Rican banking sector, T-accounts are also shown for the accounts that link Puerto Rico to the United States economy—namely, balances "due from" and "due to" United States banks and balances due to the federal government—and a T-account is shown for "local" demand deposits of Puerto Rican banks.

A similar set of accounts is shown for the United States non-bank sectors and for United States banks, with one difference. There is no account for the deposits of United States private firms in Puerto Rican banks because we assume there are none. A small number of transactions

Table 6

Accounting Framework for Transactions between Puerto Rico and the United States

PUERTO RICO				UNITED STATES			
Puerto Rican Private Non-Bank Sector		Puerto Rican Banks		United States Banks		United States Private Non-Bank Sector	
Balances with Puerto Rican Banks		Due from U.S. Banks		Due to Puerto Rican Banks		Balances with United States Banks	
Debit	Credit	Debit	Credit	Debit	Credit	Debit	Credit
A	G	A	G	G	A	G	A
C	I	E	K	K	E	H	B
		M	N	N	M	K	E
			O	O		L	F

Balances with U.S. Banks		Due to U.S. Government		Due to Puerto Rican Firms and Government	
Debit	Credit	Debit	Credit	Debit	Credit
B	H	C	I	H	B
		D	J	L	F
		N	M		
		O			

Puerto Rican Public Sector (Government and Public Authorities)		Demand Deposits (local)		Other Accounts (Domestic)		United States Government	
Balances with Puerto Rican Banks						Balances with Puerto Rican Banks	
Debit	Credit	Debit	Credit	Debit	Credit	Debit	Credit
D	J	G	A	A	G	I	C
E	K	I	C	B	H	J	D
		J	D	E	K	M	N
		K	E	F	L		O
				M*	N*		
					O*		

Balances with U.S. Banks						Balances with Federal Reserve Banks	
Debit	Credit					Debit	Credit
F	L					N	M
						O	

* Reserve Account with Federal Reserve Banks.

NOTE: Letters in the above T-accounts refer to transaction types defined in the accompanying text.

may in fact go through such accounts, but there is reason to believe the amount is insignificant.[9]

United States commercial banks have some deposits in Puerto Rican banks, and some transactions are cleared through these accounts. The moneyflows figures given in Chapter II include estimates for these transactions, as supplied by the Puerto Rican banks.

We can now trace some "typical" transactions through this accounting framework and show how information accumulates in banking records when payments are made to and from Puerto Rico. We will describe the detailed accounting entries for a few transactions and then list the others more briefly.

1. Suppose Puerto Rican firms sell merchandise to United States firms, receiving payment in the form of a check drawn on a United States bank. Typically, the Puerto Rican firm deposits the check in its Puerto Rican bank account. We have four accounting entries in each economy, as follows:

Puerto Rico	*United States*
Firm: Dr. Cash in Bank	Firm: Dr. Purchases
Cr. Sales	Cr. Cash in Bank
Bank: Dr. Deposit in	Bank: Dr. Firm's Demand
N.Y. Bank	Deposit
Cr. Firm's Demand	Cr. Due to P.R.
Deposit	Bank

2. Suppose Puerto Rican firms buy merchandise from United States firms, making payment in the form of a check on a Puerto Rican bank. Typically, the United States firm deposits the check in its United States bank account. Again, we have four entries in each economy:

9. As already mentioned, we treat Puerto Rican branches and subsidiaries of U.S. firms as Puerto Rican residents, and *their* deposit balances in Puerto Rican banks are included in the Puerto Rican non-bank private sector. The text discussion refers to U.S. firms, not Puerto Rican residents, which may keep bank balances in Puerto Rican banks.

Puerto Rico	United States
Firm: Dr. Purchases	Firm: Dr. Cash in Bank
Cr. Cash in Bank	Cr. Sales
Bank: Dr. Firm's Demand	Bank: Dr. Due to P.R.
Deposit	Bank
Cr. Deposit in	Cr. Firm's Demand
N.Y. Bank	Deposit

3. Suppose Puerto Rican individuals receive social security pensions in the form of treasury checks which they deposit in Puerto Rican bank accounts. Now we have four entries in the Puerto Rican economy and two entries in the United States economy:

Puerto Rico	United States
Individual:	
Dr. Cash in Bank	
Cr. Income Received	Treasury:
	Dr. Social Security
Bank: Dr. Treasurer's	Expenditure
General Account	Cr. Deposit in
Cr. Individual Demand Deposit	P.R. Bank

4. Suppose Puerto Rican firms pay social security taxes to the federal government by drawing checks on their deposits in Puerto Rican banks. Again, we have four entries in the Puerto Rican economy and two in the United States economy:

Puerto Rico	United States
Firm: Dr. Expenses	Treasury:
Cr. Cash in Bank	Dr. Deposit in
Bank: Dr. Individual Demand Deposit	P.R. Bank
Cr. Treasurer's	Cr. Social Security
General Account	Income

It can be seen that various "payments circuits" may be used, depending on whether the connecting bank accounts are held by the non-bank transactors in one economy in the banks of the other, or whether each region's non-bank transactors hold bank accounts in banks of their own region. On the basis of business custom and the institutional structure, we list below the chief types of transactions that involve payments through the banking system:

TRANSACTION TYPES

Receipts of Puerto Rico from United States

A. Received by P.R. firms from U.S. firms, accomplished by check drawn on U.S. bank and deposited in P.R. bank.

B. Received by P.R. firms from U.S. firms, accomplished by check drawn on U.S. bank and deposited in U.S. bank account by P.R. firm.

C. Received by P.R. firms from U.S. government, accomplished by treasury check charged to Treasurer's General Accounts in P.R. banks and deposited in P.R. bank by recipient.

D. Received by P.R. government from U.S. government, accomplished by treasury check charged to Treasurer's General Accounts in P.R. banks and deposited in P.R. bank by recipient.

E. Received by P.R. government from U.S. firms, accomplished by check drawn on U.S. bank and deposited in P.R. bank.

F. Received by P.R. government from U.S. firms, accomplished by check drawn on U.S. bank and deposited in U.S. bank by P.R. government. (As is done, for example, by public authorities in Puerto Rico.)

Payments from Puerto Rico to the United States

G. Payment from P.R. firms to U.S. firms, made by check drawn on P.R. bank and deposited in U.S. bank by recipient.

H. Payment from P.R. firms to U.S. firms, made by check drawn on U.S. bank account and deposited in U.S. bank by recipient.

I. Payment from P.R. firms to U.S. government,

made by checks drawn on P.R. bank and deposited in Treasurer's General Accounts (or in Tax and Loan Accounts).

J. Payment from P.R. government to U.S. government, made by checks drawn on P.R. bank and deposited in Treasurer's General Accounts (or in Tax and Loan Accounts).

K. Payment from P.R. government to U.S. firms, made by checks drawn on P.R. banks and deposited in U.S. banks by recipients.

L. Payment from P.R. government to U.S. firms, made by checks drawn on U.S. banks and deposited in U.S. banks by recipients. (As is done, for example, by public authorities in Puerto Rico.)

Other Transactions (actually involve two-way payment)

M. U.S. Treasury "restorations." Transfers of funds from U.S. Treasury account with Federal Reserve banks to replenish Treasurer's General Accounts with P.R. banks. Accomplished by transfer of funds to accounts of P.R. banks with their New York correspondents.

N. U.S. Treasury transfers to Federal Reserve banks from Treasurer's General Accounts. Accomplished by transfer of funds to Federal Reserve banks by charging accounts of P.R. banks with their New York correspondents.

O. U.S. Treasury transfers to Federal Reserve banks from Tax and Loan Accounts. Accomplished by transfer of funds to Federal Reserve banks by charging accounts of P.R. banks with their N.Y. correspondents. (This item also forms part of I and J.)

In Table 6, representing the accounting framework, we have added letters A through O to denote entries for each of the transaction types listed above.[10] Basically, our objective is to obtain the total value of payments made for each of these transaction types. For all except a few of them, the pertinent figures will be found in the records of Puerto Rican banks. This fact makes the task feasible,

10. For the non-bank transactors, only one side of the accounting entry is shown—namely, the one affecting the deposit balance of the transactor.

since we can seek information from eleven banks but not from thousands of firms and individuals.

Once the estimates for each transaction type are obtained, they can be used to fill in our payments matrix as shown in Table 7. This gives us a complete statement of the flow of funds to and from Puerto Rico via the banking system, classified by private and government sectors. It is then necessary to add currency movements, money orders, and other non-bank transfers in order to obtain the total flow of funds into and out of Puerto Rico.

Table 7

Matrix of Payments between Puerto Rico and the United States

		U.S. Govt.	U.S. Private Sector	Total U.S.
Puerto Rican Private Sector (incl. banks)	Payments to:	I+M	G+H+N+O	I+M+G+H+N+O
	Receipts from:	C+N+O	A+B+M	C+N+O+A+B+M
Puerto Rican Government and Public Authorities	Payments to:	J	K+L	J+K+L
	Receipts from:	D	E+F	D+E+F
Total Puerto Rican Economy	Payments to:	I+M+J	G+H+N+O+K+L	I+M+G+H+N+O+J+K+L
	Receipts from:	C+N+O+D	A+B+M+E+F	C+N+O+A+B+M+D+E+F

NOTE: Letters refer to transaction types described in the accompanying text and placed in an accounting framework in Table 6, above.

Now let us examine the availability of figures for the various payments made through the banking system. For this purpose we reproduce in Table 8 the three accounts which link the Puerto Rican and United States economies: interbank accounts, United States Treasury accounts in Puerto Rican banks, and Puerto Rican private and governmental accounts in United States banks. Availability of data for each transaction type is indicated in Table 8.

1. Interbank accounts. Total debits and credits to their correspondent accounts have been supplied by the Puerto Rican banks. Records of the Commonwealth

Table 8

Availability of Data for Bank Accounts Linking Puerto Rico and the United States

PUERTO RICAN BANKS					
Due from United States Banks					
A *		G *			
E Available		K Available			
M Available		N Available			
		O Available			
Total Available		Total Available			
			UNITED STATES COMMERCIAL BANKS		
Due to United States Government			Due to Puerto Rican Firms and Government		
C *	I *		H Not available	B Not available	
D Available	J Available		L Partially avail-	F Partially avail-	
N Available	M Available		able	able	
O Available					
Total Available	Total Available				

* Can be calculated as a residual.
NOTE: Letters in the above T-accounts refer to transaction types defined in the accompanying text.

Treasury and public authorities enable us to identify Commonwealth government transactions (E and K), and records of the United States Treasurer's General Accounts enable us to identify federal government transactions that also appear in the interbank clearings (M, N, and O). Thus by subtraction we can estimate transactions of the private sector (A and G).

2. United States Treasury accounts. Monthly reports on activity in these accounts provide figures for total debits and credits and for transfers to and from the mainland— i.e., M, N, and O. Transactions with the Commonwealth government (D and J) can be obtained from records of the

Commonwealth Treasury, and we can then obtain transactions with the private sector (C and I) by subtraction.

3. The Commonwealth Treasury has an accounting system in which all payments and receipts are classified by economic sector. One of these sectors is the federal government. Two others, "U.S.–Private" and "Rest of World," are combined to form our category of "RoW Private Sector."[11] In addition to transactions identified through this sectoral classification, we have also obtained the figures for transactions in the investment account of the Commonwealth government and for transactions of the municipalities and public authorities.

4. Balances with mainland banks. This is the most troublesome area. We can obtain the transactions of public authorities (L and F), but we cannot obtain information from the banks about the volume of transactions in accounts held in mainland banks by private firms and individuals. This information must come from the firms and individuals themselves, and complete coverage of so many reporting units is beyond our reach. However, on the basis of numerous discussions of this matter with bankers and businessmen in Puerto Rico, we conclude that the amounts involved are small, relative to the gross moneyflows exhibited in Table 6. Convenience, tax treatment, equal safety (Commonwealth banks are members of FDIC), and removal of exchange charges have led most businesses in Puerto Rico to use insular bank accounts.

Further evidence that transactions through mainland balances (and intra-firm accounting transfers) are relatively small is provided by analysis of merchandise trade. Firms that are likely to use mainland balances (or intra-firm accounting transfers) are primarily those which import materials into Puerto Rico for processing or assembly and then ship the finished product back to the mainland. They

11. I am indebted to Evaristo Ríos and Angel Negrón of the Commonwealth Treasury Bureau of Accounts for their kind assistance to me and for their explanations of accounting practices.

are both importers and exporters. Importing firms, such as the large retailers, have no source of external income, and while they may keep a mainland balance, they must replenish it from sales revenues generated in Puerto Rico. Transfers of funds from Puerto Rico to replenish the mainland balance *will* appear in our estimates because such transfers will be made through Puerto Rican banks and their mainland correspondents. Exporting firms (which do not import much directly) will similarly find it necessary to transfer funds to Puerto Rico to pay local expenses. These transfers will also appear in our estimates. Thus, as mentioned above, it is the new Fomento-attracted[12] manufacturing firm that is likely to find it convenient to use mainland bank balances or intra-firm accounting transfers. However, most of these firms desire to claim exemption from federal tax on their Puerto Rican operations, and they are anxious to provide an accounting and contractual basis for separating net income of the Puerto Rican plant. For this reason most of them *sell* parts and materials to the Puerto Rican plant and buy back the finished component. To emphasize this transaction, in most cases the Puerto Rican plant has its own bank account in a Puerto Rican bank.

Of course there are many different practices in this area, but on the basis of an examination of export composition it seems likely that less than 20 per cent of the proceeds of merchandise exports were deposited directly in mainland banks. This would mean no more than $130 million in 1960, or about 3 per cent of gross receipts in that year (from Table 1.)

To summarize, payments to and from Puerto Rico can be made in the following ways:

1. Transactions that clear through "due from" accounts of Puerto Rican banks with RoW banks.

---

12. "Fomento" is the popular name for the Economic Development Administration.

2. Transactions that clear through "due to" accounts of Puerto Rican banks, held for RoW banks.

3. Transactions with federal government through Treasurer's General Accounts and tax and loan accounts in Puerto Rican banks.

4. Transactions made through bank accounts held directly in RoW banks by (a) Puerto Rican firms and individuals, or (b) Puerto Rican government agencies.

5. Currency movements.

6. Money orders.

7. Intra-firm accounting transfers.

We have adequate or good coverage of all of these forms of payments except 4a and 7. There is some question whether intra-firm accounting transfers should be treated as payments in the first place, but in any case we have seen some reasons to believe that the amount of such transfers is relatively small. We also have reason to believe that mainland bank accounts of private firms (4a) are not used to make payments on a large scale. Therefore, we conclude that the estimates given in Chapter II constitute the great bulk of total flows of funds between Puerto Rico and the rest of the world.

CHAPTER III

BALANCE-OF-PAYMENTS APPROACH

We have said above that we shall treat Puerto Rico for some purposes as if she were a separate nation in order to utilize international trade analogies for analysis of her balance of payments. This treatment may require a word of explanation, especially since the United States dollar is also the Puerto Rican currency.

When two separate national currencies are connected with a fixed exchange rate, orderly procedures for the transfer or exchange of funds from one currency to the other are required. The reserves of B (a sterling country) may be held in gold, provided A (a dollar country) is willing to buy gold on fixed terms; or B's reserves may be held in the form of dollar demand deposits at A-banks.[1] In the latter case, payments from A-citizens to B-citizens are accomplished through the banking system and the net result is that the demand liabilities of B-banks go up, as do their deposits in A-banks, while A-banks transfer deposit liabilities from A-citizens to B-banks. In terms of balance sheets, changes occur (assume a payment of $400, with $4 = £1), as indicated in the table on page 46.

As long as B-banks possess sufficient demand balances in A-banks, and remain willing to accept increases in such balances, payments to and from A and B can readily be accomplished. It is when the demand balance of B-banks in A-banks begins to run low (or when B's gold stock is low) that difficulties arise for B-citizens making money

1. Many other institutional arrangements may, of course, exist; here we wish merely to state the problem in a simple form.

	A-banks		B-banks	
Dr.	Cr.	Dr.	Cr.
	Demand De-posit, domestic −$400	Deposit in A-bank +£100	Demand De-posits, domes-tic +£100
	Demand De-posit, B-banks +$400		

payments to A. Under a flexible exchange-rate system, the pressure on B-reserves of dollars would cause the price of A-dollars to rise, but when exchange rates are fixed by law the pressure may be handled by invoking some form of administrative rationing or by policy measures that aim to reduce the pressure.

This brief description is given so that analogies with the Puerto Rican case can be pointed out in a familiar setting. Monetary gold movements do not occur between the United States and Puerto Rico, and both economies use United States dollars as the monetary unit. We will therefore treat this relation as a fixed exchange rate with a par of unity. As described in Chapter II above, payments from United States residents to Puerto Rican residents are effected through the banking system, with the "reserves" of Puerto Rican banks (demand balances in New York correspondent banks) rising at the same time. Similarly, payments from Puerto Rican residents and firms to United States payees are ordinarily made with checks drawn on Puerto Rican banks. Such checks cause the "reserves" of Puerto Rican banks to fall, along with the fall in local deposit liabilities. In terms of balance sheets, these two transactions appear as follows:

Payment from United States to Puerto Rico			
U.S. Banks		**Puerto Rican Banks**	
Dr.	*Cr.* Demand Deposits, domestic −$100 Demand Deposits, Puerto Rican bank +$100	*Dr.* Deposit in N.Y. bank +$100	*Cr.* Demand Deposits, domestic +$100

Payment from Puerto Rico to United States			
U.S. Banks		**Puerto Rican Banks**	
Dr.	*Cr.* Demand Deposits, domestic +$200 Demand Deposits, Puerto Rican bank −$200	*Dr.* Deposit in N.Y. bank −$200	*Cr.* Demand Deposits, domestic −$200

As before, payments can readily be made between the two economies as long as Puerto Rican banks have adequate reserves (demand balances in New York banks) and if they are willing to accept additional balances in New York banks. They will ordinarily be willing to accept balances in New York banks because of the wide range of opportunities open to them to reinvest such funds and because such balances constitute increases in reserves that permit domestic loan expansion. Therefore, the real question is whether or not Puerto Rican banks will have sufficient balances in New York banks to cover payments being made from Puerto Rico to the mainland.

To illustrate the process of money payments to and from the island, let us now examine two hypothetical examples. We are here chiefly interested in the monetary mechanism, but it will also be necessary to introduce some assumptions about the flow of money income. Suppose, first, that Puerto Rico received $25 million of long-term capital through the sale of Puerto Rican Water Resources Authority bonds in the New York market, the funds to be used for construction of a new electric steam plant. (We could equally well suppose that a mainland firm had decided to build a new plant in Puerto Rico, allocating $25 million for the purpose.) When the bond proceeds are turned over to the PRWRA, let us suppose the check is deposited by the latter in a Puerto Rican bank account,[2] thus increasing commercial bank demand liabilities (deposits) in Puerto Rico and simultaneously increasing "reserves" in New York banks. The immediate response of the Puerto Rican bank will probably be to use part of the increase in its New York balance to buy short-term securities in the New York market. As construction of the steam plant proceeds, Puerto Rican banks will experience adverse clearings because checks will be drawn to pay for

2. Actually, PRWRA is one of the few authorities that maintains its own account in a mainland bank. This makes no essential difference, however, for we will simply include such balances as part of the "reserves" of Puerto Rico.

materials and equipment bought directly from mainland suppliers and because the purchase of domestic factor services will lead to a secondary increase in imports and other external payments. Thus the original increment to reserves will gradually be reduced, causing banks to sell short-term securities in order to meet the adverse clearing balance. If the marginal propensity to save is positive, not all of the initial $25 million will be drained away in direct and induced imports. A fraction of this sum will remain in the possession of Puerto Rican banks, permitting them to expand their loans and deposits by a (small) multiple of the residual.

A numerical example is a convenient way to illustrate the point. Suppose $10 million of the original $25 million is spent for direct mainland purchases, with the remaining $15 million spent for local materials and services. Assuming a marginal propensity to consume domestic products (c_d) of 0.4, a marginal propensity to consume imports (c_m) of 0.5, and a marginal propensity to save (s) of 0.1, we have a multiplier of $1\frac{2}{3}$, or $k = \left(\dfrac{1}{s+c_m}\right) = \dfrac{1.0}{.6} = 1.66\frac{2}{3}$.[3]

This multiplier applies to the initial increment in *domestic* expenditures; that is, in our example it applies to the $15 million used to buy Puerto Rican materials and services. The reader will have observed that we are ignoring the foreign repercussions usually allowed for in discussions of the foreign-trade multiplier. We make no allowance for the effect of this transaction on United States incomes and United States purchases from Puerto Rico. However, it seems likely that this effect will be very small, and its omission makes little difference in our results.

In this example, then, we find that the change in Puerto Rican income, ΔY, is:

$$\Delta Y = 15\left(\frac{1}{s+c_m}\right) = 15\left(\frac{1.0}{.1+.5}\right) = 25.$$

3. Foreign repercussions are assumed to be zero. The propensities assumed here are for illustrative purposes only, but they are very similar to those calculated on the basis of Puerto Rican experience in a later section.

Similarly, the increases in imports, ΔM, and saving, ΔS, are:

$$\Delta M = c_m(\Delta Y) = .5(25) = 12.5$$
$$\Delta S = s(\Delta Y) = .1(25) = 2.5.$$

The simple form of the multiplier used here allows for the influence of the marginal propensity to import for consumption (c_m).

Thus, we observe that, of the original $25 million of external funds, $22.5 million $(10.0 + 12.5)$ will have been used up through adverse clearings, leaving Puerto Rican banks with increased external assets of $2.5 million. Domestic deposit liabilities will also have risen by the same amount, $2.5 million. If we assume that commercial banks expand loans for investment purposes to the limit of their ability, and if the above ratios and spending propensities hold for these domestic loans of Puerto Rican banks, they will then be able to increase domestic loans by about $2.14 million, of which about $1.96 million will be drained away in adverse clearings. In the end, banks will be left with additional New York deposits of $0.54 million, and their demand deposits will be increased by about $2.68 million. These results are obtained by applying the usual formulae for the potential expansion of loans and deposits, given an increase in the amount of reserves. Our calculations are significantly affected, however, by the allowance we must make for the "leakage" through imports from the rest of the world.

Letting A stand for excess reserves, ΔL for potential loan expansion, and ΔDD for potential deposit expansion, the multiple-expansion formulae in this case are:

$$\Delta L = A[1.0 + 0.06\tfrac{2}{3} + (0.06\tfrac{2}{3})^2 + \ldots]$$
$$= A\left(\frac{1.0}{1.0 - .06\tfrac{2}{3}}\right) = A(1\tfrac{1}{14}) = A(1.07142\ldots).$$
$$\Delta DD = .08\tfrac{1}{3}\, A\left(\frac{1}{1.0 - .06\tfrac{2}{3}}\right) = .08\tfrac{1}{3}\,(A)(1.07142\ldots)$$
$$\approx .089(A).$$

To derive the formula for loan expansion, we assume that banks, finding themselves with excess reserves, make additional loans in an amount equal to their initial excess reserves. For convenience we also assume that these loans are made for investment purposes, and that one-half of the sum lent is spent directly for imports. The remaining half is spent for domestic goods and services, thus generating an increase in domestic income and a further increase in imports. These two "leakages" amount to $91\frac{2}{3}$ per cent of the new deposits (based on the propensities assumed in the text, above), leaving $8\frac{1}{3}$ per cent of the new deposit. Against this remaining deposit, required reserves of 20 per cent must be held. Therefore, after the first "round" of new loans, excess reserves equal $6\frac{2}{3}$ per cent of the original amount $[8\frac{1}{3}\% - 20\%(8\frac{1}{3}\%) = 6\frac{2}{3}\%]$. Thus we generate a series: $1.0 + .06\frac{2}{3} + (.06\frac{2}{3})^2 + \ldots = \dfrac{1.0}{1.0 - .06\frac{2}{3}} = 15/14$ $= 1.07142.\ldots$

The formula for deposit expansion is then obtained directly. As we have seen, Puerto Rican banks retain $8\frac{1}{3}$ per cent of new deposits initially created by loan expansion. The remainder of the new deposits, $91\frac{2}{3}$ per cent, are lost through adverse clearings. Thus Puerto Rican deposits rise by $8\frac{1}{3}$ per cent of loan expansion, or: $\Delta DD = .08\frac{1}{3} A (1.07142\ldots) = 0.089(A)$.

In this example, the "multiplier" for the multiple expansion of bank deposits based upon a given initial excess reserve is slightly under 0.09. If allowance were made for increases in currency in circulation, we might find that Puerto Rican banks can in effect lend only the amount of their excess reserves, which would put "all commercial banks" in Puerto Rico on about the same basis as a single commercial bank in the United States as far as power to create money is concerned. Upon reflection, this may seem to be a rather obvious and unsurprising conclusion. Certainly we would not expect the banks in a single city, such as Denver, to be able to expand loans and deposits by six or seven times their initial excess reserves; and in many respects Puerto Rico may be regarded as a "city" (or a small region), tightly integrated with the larger economy of which it is a part.

Although this conclusion may be unsurprising, perhaps we should mention its relevance to a small nation whose marginal propensity to import is large. The usual treatment of the monetary aspects of balance-of-payments adjustment proceeds on the assumption that an inflow of gold (or other increment in exchange reserves) will permit an expansion of the domestic money supply by a multiple whose size is determined by the domestic reserve ratio. The subsequent increase in prices and incomes will then tend to bring the inflow of gold to an end. While this is partly a matter of timing, our analysis suggests that in a small nation closely linked to the external economy the domestic money supply will expand by only a fraction of the increment in reserves, even though a fractional reserve (such as 20 per cent) is used in the banking system. There is an interplay between monetary expansion and income expansion that is not usually allowed for in discussions of the adjustment mechanism in the balance of payments.

The size of the various multipliers is of some interest. Based on the figures chosen in the above example, income expansion arising from the investment financed by capital inflow is $25 million, making the investment multiplier $(\Delta Y/\Delta I)$ exactly unity. Adding the income expansion resulting from the rise in bank loans ($2.14 million), income rises but little more than the amount of capital inflow. The money supply in Puerto Rico rises by $2.68 million and, if we compare this to the initial increase in mainland funds of $25 million, the money-creation multiplier is only 0.11. Thus the inflow of long-term capital permits a small increase of the Puerto Rican money supply. Through connecting bank balances and other "points of contact"— especially short-term dollar securities held by Puerto Rican banks—the payments process operates in an orderly fashion. It does not, however, involve the process of cumulative expansion of income and money supply (that is, a magnification of the original impact) that is usually contemplated in this theory. In a fractional reserve case, the increase in bank reserves is usually said to permit an increase in the money supply that is approximately equal to $1/R$ times the new reserves, where R is the reserve ratio. In our case this would mean the $25 million of reserves would support a total increase in the money supply of $125 million, instead of the $2.7 million we actually found in our example.

Because the strain on the payments mechanism is greater for an outflow than for an inflow, let us also examine a case in which capital inflow declines below its former level. Suppose capital inflow falls by $25 million and domestic investment also drops by this amount. Now the changes in income and other variables in our previous example are for the most part simply reversed. Income falls by a total of $25 million, with direct and induced declines in imports of $22.5 million and in saving of $2.5 million. The fall in effective demand for domestically-produced goods and services is accompanied by decreases in income and employment. Wages and prices come under downward pressure. How serious this will be will depend in part on the ability to export the goods formerly produced for domestic use and on the ease with which resources can be transferred to export industries. We cannot enter into these questions at this point, but it may be noted that there is little reason to be optimistic about the short-run flexibility of supply in this respect.

Because of the rapid fall in imports, as investment and consumption decline in Puerto Rico, banks would not experience heavy adverse clearings and outward payments. The small volume of adverse clearings to be expected could easily be met by the banks through sales of liquid assets and by drawing on lines of credit. The loss of reserves will require a small contraction in deposit liabilities ($2.7 million) unless the banks are willing to hold a smaller ratio of secondary reserves to total assets than they held before. As in the expansion example, we do not find a "multiple contraction" of money and income as is usually contemplated in theoretical discussions of this process in international trade.

The price and income effects of conventional analysis are operating here, although the initial force is not magnified in the process of adjustment. In this case we are concentrating on the income effect and, assuming that wages and prices are inflexible, external payments are restrained through the creation of an increased amount of unemployment in the Puerto Rican economy. Except to the extent that it can itself borrow larger sums in the United States financial markets, the Commonwealth government can do little through direct action to attack the unemployment. However, the opportunity for migration does permit idle workers to remove themselves from the Puerto Rican economy. Since inflowing capital does not enter Puerto Rico primarily to produce for the local market, the presence of increasing unemployment of labor will not necessarily operate as a restraint on such inflow. Failure of domestic resources to be fully utilized with a given set of prices and production opportunities will, even in the absence of price flexibilities, produce equilibrating tendencies. Labor is stimulated to move out, while capital inflows are not discouraged. To the extent that labor moves out and capital continues to come in, the disequilibrium is steadily eliminated. The payments process is also facilitated by these movements—at least by the capital inflows.[4]

Purely for expository purposes, it may be of interest to

4. This process is complicated, however, by cyclical patterns. When the U.S. is in a recession, direct capital investment in Puerto Rico decreases, while

consider the more drastic case in which a massive shift occurs in expectations about the prospects for the Puerto Rican economy. Suppose, for example, that the end of tax exemption plus rising wage minimums were to cause mainland firms to lose interest in Puerto Rican operations, with the result that they ceased making new investments and even attempted to sell their present assets. Firms and individuals would begin to withdraw funds from Puerto Rican banks and to transfer them to the mainland, and they would begin to sell Puerto Rican assets, also attempting to transfer the money proceeds to mainland accounts. These actions would produce adverse clearing balances that would reduce the New York balances of Puerto Rican banks, and the latter would then be forced to sell securities and perhaps to rediscount commercial paper with their correspondents. At the same time new loans would have been curtailed in Puerto Rico because banks would have lost reserves. As loans and deposits were reduced the pressure on reserves would ease. However, both the external drain of funds and the contraction of local lending would operate to reduce the volume of deposits in Puerto Rican banks. Such a reduction of the money supply would occur automatically, and one of the implications of the foregone monetary autonomy is that the Commonwealth government could take no direct action to prevent it.[5]

If the calamity we are postulating became more wide-

---

at the same time employment opportunities for Puerto Rican emigrants on the U.S. mainland decline. These two factors may combine to reduce employment in Puerto Rico and thus to produce an especially difficult situation. Both alleviating responses are thwarted.

5. There are actions that the government could take to ease the pressure on banks, however. For one thing, the Government Development Bank could rediscount some local paper, thus making available its New York funds. Second, the Commonwealth Treasurer could accept local claims as collateral against government deposits, thus freeing the sizable bank holdings of U.S. securities for meeting the external drain. Cf. Biagio Di Venuti, *Money and Banking in Puerto Rico* (Río Piedras: University of Puerto Rico, 1950), p. 65.

spread, property values would no doubt fall, and some commercial paper (even short-term "self-liquidating" paper) held by the banks would become uncollectible. Commonwealth bonds would fall in price, causing losses to the holders upon sale. Refunding issues would be difficult to market. Nevertheless, the banks should still be able to meet the demands upon them. Branches of United States and Canadian banks could of course draw upon outside resources, and if necessary their entire portfolios could be taken over by the home office in order to meet the demands of depositors for mainland funds.[6] The real question concerns the ability of Commonwealth-chartered banks to survive. Assuming that no help were forthcoming from the Federal Reserve System or from the United States Treasury, these banks would find it difficult to maintain "convertibility" into mainland funds, but they would fail only if a truly catastrophic alteration occurred in the economic climate.[7] They could meet sizable drains by rediscounting paper with mainland correspondents, utilizing lines of credit, and selling their holdings of securities. If they did become insolvent, the Federal Deposit Insurance Corporation would enter the picture. Its payments would represent an added supply of mainland funds.

Another factor which would tend to alleviate the crisis is that as external owners of capital assets (such as Puerto Rican plants) put them up for sale, no strain would necessarily be put on the payments mechanism because the buyer would probably also be an external resident. That is, at *some* price other United States firms or individuals would buy the capital assets, probably paying in checks drawn on United States bank accounts. Only if Puerto Rican residents bought the plants would Puerto Rican banks be faced with the necessity of "converting" local funds into New York funds.

6. Such branch banks hold 40 per cent of commercial bank assets.

7. This statement, of course, does not mean that a particular bank may not fail at any time because of unwise loans and other errors of judgment by management.

We may conclude that there is in fact little prospect of a balance-of-payments crisis in Puerto Rico, but this is a topic that will be further discussed below.

After the preliminary discussion of the monetary links between the Puerto Rican and United States economies, we now turn to an examination of the Puerto Rican balance of payments in the postwar period.

Chapter IV

POSTWAR BALANCE-OF-PAYMENTS EXPERIENCE

Puerto Rico has been exposed in the last twenty years to external influences that have required sizable economic adjustments in her domestic economy and in her balance of payments. Futhermore, changes initiated at home have also had a large influence on the balance of payments. Throughout this series of economic "disturbances," no question of convertibility has ever been raised, and not even a mild balance-of-payments crisis has been overtly recognized to exist. In other words, the institutional structure has been able to handle the required adjustments, which are sometimes quite drastic, with no visible signs of strain. We shall try to show how and why these adjustments occurred.

In this chapter we shall briefly describe the major economic events of the postwar period, with emphasis upon their relation to, and impact upon, the balance of payments. In the next chapter some analysis and interpretation of the observed experience will be offered.

Although our chief interest is in the period 1946 to 1959, a summary of wartime experience will be helpful. Puerto Rican income received a strong stimulus from the growth of federal military expenditures in the island and from the war-induced expansion of exports. Federal expenditures on insular goods and services—the gross product concept—rose from $23 million in 1940 to $124 million in 1944 and to $137 million in 1945.[1] In the latter years this

1. *Economic Development of Puerto Rico, 1941-50, 1951-60*, Commonwealth of Puerto Rico, Planning Board, 1951, p. 162. Years refer to fiscal years ending June 30, here and throughout this study.

item comprised about one-fifth of gross insular product. "Receipts" from the federal government, as listed in the balance of payments, amounted to \$159 million in 1944 and \$157 million in 1945, or about one-half of total current-account credits.[2] At the same time, merchandise exports (primarily rum and sugar) rose sharply under the stimulus of wartime demand.

These large increases in external spending for insular goods and services swiftly increased Puerto Rican income. The high marginal propensity to import carried imports to record levels and, in merchandise trade alone, the island experienced large debit balances. This in itself was unusual, for Puerto Rico had had an export balance on merchandise account in nearly all years from 1900 to 1940. Even so, imports of goods and services were restrained by wartime scarcities and shipping shortages. Under the force of these restraints, the total current account in the Puerto Rican balance of payments showed a surplus during the war years, and residents, firms, and government accumulated sizable amounts of liquid assets. These accumulations amounted to about \$380 million for the period 1942 to 1946[3] and were primarily in the form of United States securities, balances with mainland banks, and currency. The Commonwealth government also enjoyed a surplus of receipts over expenditures, which arose in large measure from the windfall of excise tax refunds on rum shipped to the mainland.[4] The significance of this accumulation may

2. R. L. Sammons and B. H. Cestero, *The Balance of External Payments of Puerto Rico, 1942-46* (Río Piedras: University of Puerto Rico, 1948). There are several differences between the current account and gross product concepts, but in these years the chief difference is that the balance-of-payments concept includes tax rebates on rum and tobacco shipped to the mainland and federal transfer payments.

3. Sammons and Cestero, *Balance of External Payments.*

4. "Between 1941 and 1946, remissions to Puerto Rico of Federal excise tax collections on the sale of Puerto Rican rum in the United States amounted to about \$160 million more than 'normal' expectations, an amount five times the 1940 budget of the Insular Government." H. C. Barton, Jr., "Puerto Rico's Industrial Development Program, 1942-1960," a paper presented at the Center for International Affairs, Harvard University, October 29, 1959.

be suggested by the fact that it was larger than the estimate for insular gross product in 1941, and two-thirds as large as the 1945 gross product. Such an amount, in liquid assets, constituted a tidy nest egg on which to base an economic development effort. A large part of this liquid reserve was in the hands of the Commonwealth government.

Being unable to spend these monies for useful purposes during the war, the government prudently accumulated stocks of liquid assets. Simultaneously, the banks found their rising deposit liabilities matched by rising balances in mainland banks, and, being unable to expand local loans on a sound basis, they purchased large amounts of United States securities. Individuals increased their holdings of bank balances, United States savings bonds, and currency. Some of the increased currency holdings in Puerto Rico must be treated as necessary additions to the money supply and not as temporary foreign exchange "reserves." In this respect, Puerto Rico is similar to a country on the full gold standard—all money in circulation outside the banks is itself 100 per cent acceptable in international exchange. This is, of course, a point of strength, since contractions in currency *per se* resulting from increased demand for foreign exchange will create no exchange difficulties. To the extent that her money supply is composed of currency, then, Puerto Rico has a 100 per cent reserve system.

The rise in commercial bank holdings of United States securities is illustrated by the increase in their "bonds and investments" from $4 million in 1940 to $160 million in 1945.[5]

External influences clearly dominated the Puerto Rican economy and fixed the pattern of its balance of payments during the war years. In brief, heavy sales of goods and services to the federal government and to the mainland,

5. File reports in the Bureau of Bank Examinations, Department of the Treasury, San Juan, Puerto Rico.

plus an increase in transfer payments from the federal government, caused a sharp increase in income and external receipts. Being unable to spend money income at the "normal" or desired rate because of limitations on import supplies and wartime controls, Puerto Rican recipients (both private and governmental) accumulated liquid assets. In balance-of-payments terminology, the current-account surplus was accompanied by an outflow of short-term capital. In the specific banking mechanism discussed above, primary increases in deposit liabilities of Puerto Rican banks were matched first by increases in mainland bank balances, but the latter were largely used to purchase United States short-term securities. The short-term capital movement was clearly the accommodating and equilibrating factor.

We shall divide the postwar period 1946 to 1959 into three parts. This is a somewhat arbitrary division, and the sub-periods overlap to some extent, but the classification is nevertheless an aid to exposition. The periods we shall use are the following:

1946-49: Current-account deficits financed by liquidation of wartime accumulations of external assets.

1950-54: Continued liquidations of external assets; beginning of inflow of long-term external capital onthe initiative of the Commonwealth government.

1955-59: Continuation of capital inflow under Commonwealth government auspices, but accompanied by a surge of private direct investment.

1946-1949

At the end of World War II, the Puerto Rican balance of payments on current account quickly turned passive. Consumption expenditures rose, but continuing supply difficulties restrained the rate of increase. Both public and private investment increased, with the largest increases occurring in the public sector as the government moved to equip the economy with badly needed social-overhead facilities. Exports continued buoyant, except for sales to the federal government, which declined in this period. This decline in federal expenditures for goods and services was in large measure offset, however, by increases in federal transfer payments to Puerto Rican residents. Changes in the classification of gross product and balance-of-payments statistics somewhat obscure the matter, but it appears that total receipts of dollars from federal sources declined slightly in this period.

At the same time, rising expenditures for consumption and investment, much of which had to be supplied through imports, led to sharply increased imports of goods and services and produced a deficit on current account in the balance of payments.

Pertinent statistics are summarized in Table 9; for greater detail see Table 14. It may be seen in Table 9 that exports of merchandise and services rose in every year from 1945 to 1949, but the sharp decline in operational disbursements of the federal government caused total current-account receipts to fall after 1946. Imports of goods and services almost doubled between 1945 and 1947, rising from $223 million to $400 million and then leveling off. The current-account balance shifted from surplus to deficit between 1946 and 1947.

The impact of this shift upon the Puerto Rican economy was eased somewhat by the rise of federal transfer payments. These payments rose from about $5 million in the early 1940's to $80 million in 1948. Much of the latter figure represented the payment of veterans' benefits, and as these benefits tapered off federal transfer payments declined only to rise again to even higher levels in the 1950's.

Vexing conceptual and definitional problems are raised by federal transfer payments, as well as by other aspects of the relationship between the federal government and the Puerto Rican economy. We have said that we wish to treat Puerto Rico "as if" she were a separate nation and thus to make use of international trade analogies. Such treatment

Table 9

Summary Balance of Payments of Puerto Rico, 1945-49[a]

(millions of dollars)

	1945	1946	1947	1948	1949
Exports of Goods and Services, total	*$276*	*$340*	*$273*	*$282*	*$294*
Merchandise and Services	174	222	226	234	246
Operational Disbursements of Federal Government	102	118	47	48	48
Imports of Goods and Services, total	*-223*	*-303*	*-400*	*-439*	*-427*
Balance of Goods and Services	*53*	*37*	*-127*	*-157*	*-133*
Unilateral Transfers, net	*12*	*25*	*63*	78	73
Private	3	2	-5	-2	2
Federal	9	23	68	80	71
Balance of Goods, Services, and Transfers	*65*	*62*	*-64*	*-79*	*-60*
Financing (each item net):					
Puerto Rican Capital:					
Short-term	-21	-33	55	25	32
Long-term	-73	-11	-20	22	14
External Capital:					
Short-term	15	- 9	- 2	13	-10
Long-term (Puerto Rican Bonds)			21	1	- 1
Long-term (Federal Agency; Mortgage Loans, etc.)	8	- 7	8	- 2	10
Long-term Direct Investment			1	6	14
Errors	7	- 1	1	14	1

a For 1945 and 1946, adjustments were made to render the figures comparable to those of later years. Specifically, excise tax refunds were put in export proceeds and federal transfer payments were removed from current account. Detail may not add because of rounding error.

SOURCES: R. L. Sammons and B. H. Cestero, *The Balance of External Payments of Puerto Rico, 1942-46* (Río Piedras: University of Puerto Rico, 1948); *The Balance of Payments of Puerto Rico, 1959*, Commonwealth of Puerto Rico, Planning Board (n.d.).

suggests that any payment from the federal government to Puerto Rico, not involving direct purchases of goods and services or the creation of a debt, should be treated as a "unilateral transfer." The trouble with this is that the term "unilateral transfer" carries a strong connotation of "donation," or free gift from one national economy to another, while many of the federal transfer payments to Puerto Rico are based on legal obligations and rights. For example, Puerto Rican veterans of service in the United States armed forces are entitled to veterans' benefits on exactly the same basis as are mainland veterans. Similarly, workers in covered employments pay social security taxes and receive benefits on the same basis as do mainland workers. The concept of "unilateral transfers" as it is ordinarily used in international accounting does not quite fit, if only because such contractual transfer payments do not arise in an important way between separate national entities. On the other hand, it may be argued that, because Puerto Rico pays no taxes to the federal treasury (except for social security taxes), her receipts under federally financed programs have the character of gifts.[6]

A different kind of issue is raised by other federal transactions—for example, the refund to the Commonwealth government of federal excise taxes levied on shipments of Puerto Rican rum and tobacco. How should these payments be treated in the balance of payments? In their original work, Sammons and Cestero included them in receipts from the federal government and listed them in the current account. Beginning with 1947, Planning Board publications treat gross receipts from rum exports (including the excise tax) as export proceeds and include this entire amount in merchandise exports. Thus the balance-of-payments statements do not now reveal that the federal government is in any way involved in this transaction. Yet if Puerto Rico were a separate nation, only the value

6. Sammons and Cestero, *Balance of External Payments*, raise this issue briefly. They say that separation of federal purchases of goods and services from unilateral transfers would involve arbitrary decisions that carry political significance, and they preferred to make no such attempt. Such a separation was later made, however, in balance-of-payments estimates made by the Planning Board. As far as I know, the rationale of this separation was never explained in published documents.

net of tax would be received as the proceeds of rum exports. This excise-tax refund seems more logically to fit the classification "transfer payment" than do veterans' benefits and the like.

In this study we shall use the classification found in the current balance of payments, although we shall occasionally reassemble the data on federal transactions in a different way. For some purposes, we shall examine the balance on current account *plus* unilateral transfers. This is done to emphasize the point that unilateral transfers received by Puerto Rico are essentially different from those included in "compensatory official financing" in early International Monetary Fund reports. In those reports, unilateral transfers were regarded as "gap fillers" or accommodating items in the balance of payments. There is no evidence that federal programs have been initiated as a means of covering a Puerto Rican balance-of-payments deficit, although federal payments do of course enable Puerto Rico to maintain a higher level of imports than she otherwise could.

To return to the 1946 to 1949 period, we have seen that the Puerto Rican current account shifted from a surplus to a deficit under the joint impact of reduced federal expenditures and increased imports. As may be seen in Table 9, the yearly net balances were as follows (millions):

	1945	*1946*	*1947*	*1948*	*1949*
Current-account balance	$ 53	37	−127	−157	−133
Unilateral transfers, net	$ 12	25	63	78	73
Current-plus-U.T. balance	$ 65	62	−64	−79	−60

The deficits beginning in fiscal year 1947 were financed by liquidating part of the wartime accumulation of external assets. This liquidation took place primarily in the banking sector, which sold United States securities in order to obtain cover for the adverse clearing balances resulting from rising import demand. Direct investment in Puerto Rico by external capitalists and insular bond issues in mainland financial markets had not yet begun on a very large scale. (An exception to the latter statement is provided by the Water Resources Authority bond issue of $21.9 million in 1947.) The pertinent figures are summarized in the "financing" section of Table 9, where it may be seen that liquidation of Puerto Rican short-term assets abroad (which include bank-held assets) provided the bulk of the funds to cover the current-account deficits in the years 1947 to 1949. The Commonwealth government also drew down its accumulated surpluses, but this did not result in much net sale of foreign assets (chiefly United States securities) because the government first drew down its deposits with Puerto Rican banks (thus forcing the banks to sell *their* United States securities) and because other governmental programs caused a marked increase in the investment account of the government during these same years.[7] There was a small net liquidation, however.

Taking the three-year period (1947-49) as a whole, the current-plus-U.T. deficit of $203 million was financed as follows:

Method of Financing Current Account Deficits, 1947-1949
(millions of dollars)

Liquidation of Puerto Rican External Assets		$128
Short-term	112	
Long-term	16	
Inflow of External Capital		58
Sale of insular bonds	21	

7. The "long-term" Puerto Rican capital item in Table 9 is dominated by government transactions. The $20 million outflow (net purchase of foreign assets) and the $22 million inflow (net sale) are simply wash transactions associated with the Water Resources Authority bond issue mentioned above. The proceeds were first invested in U.S. securities (1947) which were subsequently sold (1948).

Loans of federal agencies, mortgage
loans, etc.   21
Direct investment   16
Errors   17
                                                                              ———
Current-plus-U.T. Balance   203
Unilateral Transfers, net   214
                                                                              ———
Current-account Balance $417

It should be noted that the liquidation of external assets in the postwar period did not go nearly as far as the wartime accumulation. The Puerto Rican economy appears to have retained a net increase in external assets. One reason for this may be that an increased amount of currency was required to finance the much greater money national income. Wartime currency accumulations were in large measure retained by the economy because its transactions demand for money had shifted to the right. Other components of liquidity preference may also have increased.

While it is often difficult to determine in a specific empirical situation whether the current or capital account is "autonomous," in this case there is little doubt that the current-account changes arose from autonomous factors and induced a response in the capital account. The outflow of Puerto Rican short-term capital (the sale of external assets owned by Puerto Rican banks) was clearly an accommodating and equilibrating item in the balance of payments, just as the inflow (acquisition of these assets) had been an accommodating item during the war years.

The wartime accumulations gave Puerto Rico a breathing spell, as it were, but the economy stood at a critical juncture. Federal outlays for war purposes had not expanded productive capacity, nor had private or governmental investment been large in the war years. With expected sharp reductions in federal defense outlays and with the end of veterans' benefits, Puerto Rico faced the prospect of reverting to prewar levels of income and import capacity. This prospect was doubly unappealing because people had become accustomed to the higher level of income and because the population was now considerably larger than before (1,870,000 in 1940; 2,210,000 in 1950). A decline to prewar levels of real income would have required painful adjustments.[8] To avoid such an economic calamity, vigorous efforts were made to expand productive capacity, particularly in export industries. But essential pre-conditions of such expansion included the development of power, transport, education, and other basic facilities. The Commonwealth government undertook a bold program to develop such facilities and thus to provide the basis for the expansion of private industry and of exports. We cannot begin to describe the full developmental program; here we wish merely to note that it had two principal aspects: (1) the provision of social overhead facilities by the insular government and its public authorities, financed through bond issues in mainland capital markets, and (2) attraction of mainland direct investment through inducements, assistance, and sales promotion.[9]

1950-1954

Although it acquired momentum in the postwar period, the developmental program of the insular government had actually begun much earlier. During the Tugwell administration (which began in 1941), the Planning Board, Government Development Bank, Industrial Development Company, and several other key institutions were launched. Technicians in numerous fields were brought in to study Puerto Rican problems.

8. According to Planning Board estimates, *real* gross product in 1947 was 42 per cent above the 1940 level, and per capita real product was 22 per cent higher. *Income and Product, Puerto Rico, 1959,* Commonwealth of Puerto Rico, Planning Board, n.d.

9. For a statement of the problem, see *Economic Development of Puerto Rico, 1941-1950, 1951-1960,* and Harvey Perloff, *Puerto Rico's Economic Future* (Chicago: University of Chicago Press, 1950); for a quick view of results, see William H. Stead, *Fomento: The Economic Development of Puerto Rico* (Washington: National Planning Association, March, 1958).

The stage was therefore set for effective government action to expand capital formation and to create an economic environment attractive to private mainland investors. Public fixed investment (gross) quickly rose from negligible amounts during the war. It was financed in the beginning from the accumulated surpluses, but the insular government and its various agencies, anxious to establish and maintain a high credit rating, began to issue bonds in New York even though they still held sizable amounts of liquid assets.

Public fixed investment in the postwar period rose as follows (millions of dollars):[10]

	1947	1948	1949	1950	1951	1952	1953	1954
Commonwealth Government	$ 8	$11	$14	$20	$19	$19	$29	$28
Public Enterprises	19	28	39	39	30	51	54	44
Municipalities	1	2	2	2	2	3	3	3
	$28	$41	$55	$61	$51	$73	$86	$75
Public Investment as Percentage of Total Fixed Investment	44%	40%	48%	55%	40%	49%	54%	46%

As we have seen above, through 1949 (fiscal year) the government did not go to the mainland financial markets to any great extent, but beginning in 1950 the government began to make frequent issues of bonds in New York. In fact, the bulk of long-term capital entering Puerto Rico from 1950 to 1954 came through the purchase of bonds. At the source this was, of course, private capital, but at the point of disposition it was controlled and administered by government.

During this period commercial banks continued to expand local loans, meeting the external drain thereby induced by continuing to reduce their holdings of United States securities and other external assets. Direct investment rose in these years, and began to represent a major factor in the economy. Also important was the inflow of

10. *Income and Product, 1959.*

capital to finance housing construction; this inflow came through the purchase of mortgages—in the beginning principally those that were federally insured.

Thus the expansion of domestic investment, coupled with the revival of federal expenditures after the Korean War began, made it possible for the insular gross product to continue its upward movement. The rise of exports of goods and services was also a source of strength, and by the end of this period the output of tax-exempt firms had begun to swell the flow of exports. Net income originating in tax-exempt manufacturing firms, most of which were producing for export markets, rose as follows (millions):[11]

1947	$	1951	$ 4.2
1948		1952	7.0
1949	.6	1953	23.4
1950	1.8	1954	46.5

In Table 10 we continue the tabulation given for the previous period in Table 9. There it may be seen that imports rose somewhat faster than exports and that operational disbursements of the federal government rose to compensate for the drop in federal transfer payments, thus leaving a fluctuating "current-plus-U.T. deficit" in the balance of payments. For the entire five-year period, this deficit amounted to $276 million, financed as follows (millions):

Method of Financing Current Account Deficits, 1950-54

Puerto Rican External Assets [acquisition (−)]		− $ 45
Short-term	33	
Long-term	−78	
Inflow of External Capital		310
Short-term	47	
Sale of insular bonds	111	
Loans of federal agencies, mortgage loans, etc.	65	
Direct investment	87	
Errors		11

11. *Ibid.*, pp. 15-16.

Current-plus-U.T. Balance   276
Unilateral Transfer, net   339

Current-account Balance   615

Table 10[a]

Summary Balance of Payments of Puerto Rico, 1950-54

(millions of dollars)

	1950	1951	1952	1953	1954
Exports of Goods and Services, total	*$329*	*$386*	*$433*	*$536*	*$550*
Merchandise and Services	282	326	326	408	442
Operational Disbursements of Federal Government	47	60	107	128	108
Imports of Goods and Services, total	*−437*	*−538*	*−567*	*−629*	*−675*
Balance of Goods and Services	*−108*	*−152*	*−134*	*− 93*	*−126*
Unilateral Transfers, net	*76*	*59*	*57*	*68*	*79*
Private	2	8	12	17	17
Federal	74	51	45	51	62
Balance of Goods, Services, and Transfers	*−32*	*−93*	*−78*	*−26*	*−47*
Financing (each item net):					
Puerto Rican Capital:					
Short-term	4	12	16	− 2	3
Long-term	−18	−11	−15	−13	−21
External Capital:					
Short-term	− 1	26	21	10	− 9
Long-term (Puerto Rican Bonds)	29	22	8	7	45
Long-term (Federal Agency; Mortgage Loans, etc.)	6	24	22	6	7
Long-term Direct Investment	11	19	15	16	26
Errors	1	1	11	2	− 4

[a] Detail may not add because of rounding error.
SOURCE: *Balance of Payments of Puerto Rico, 1959*, Commonwealth of Puerto Rico, Planning Board, n.d.

While Puerto Rican short-term assets abroad were still being drawn down, it is worthy of note that long-term assets (principally United States government securities) were again accumulated in this period. Such assets were acquired primarily by the insular government,[12] which holds them as investments required by law in pension funds, in sinking funds for bond redemption, and in other investment and reserve accounts.

Inflows of capital for direct investment increased considerably over the 1946-49 period, but still remained smaller than the inflows of capital arising from the sale of bonds by insular governments.

The economic development of Puerto Rico was gathering force and momentum in this period, taking it beyond the stage of financing through wartime liquidations. Domestic capital formation rose steadily and, as we have seen, almost half of it was undertaken under public auspices. The ratio of gross domestic investment to gross insular product reached 17 per cent in this period. This vigorous economic expansion was associated with current-account deficits and was financed by inflows of long-term capital. Since the expansion and the capital inflow took place together, we cannot (and need not) designate one as the autonomous or leading factor. Had the insular government not been able to float its bonds in the New York market, much of the economic expansion would not have occurred, nor would the capital inflow have been as great. On the other hand, if the Puerto Rican drive for economic growth had been less vigorous and determined and government initiative less widely used, the capital inflow might not have occurred at all.

We present in Table 11 a summary of gross insular product in recent years, showing the major components of gross product and its rate of increase.

12. More accurately, the *known* holdings of such assets are primarily those of the insular government. Private holdings of stocks, bonds, and other external assets are very imperfectly known.

Table 11

Gross Insular Product[a] and Related Statistics—Current Dollars
(millions of dollars)

Item	Fiscal Year													
	1947	1948	1949	1950	1951	1952	1953	1954	1955	1956	1957	1958	1959	1960
Consumption Expenditures	654.0	702.0	728.4	749.5	822.6	903.0	985.6	1039.3	1097.4	1169.8	1244.5	1318.5	1424.2	1527.0
Households	579.0	622.6	635.1	663.3	724.0	791.6	866.2	910.2	957.9	1021.6	1063.7	1129.0	1216.1	1302.3
Government	74.5	79.5	93.3	86.2	98.6	111.4	119.4	129.0	139.5	148.2	180.5	189.5	208.1	224.7
Gross Domestic Investment	88.0	107.4	121.6	107.8	146.9	192.6	157.5	172.7	204.8	221.0	260.5	280.0	318.6	339.6
Change in Inventories	25.2	7.3	5.7	-0.7	19.7	42.2	-1.5	9.4	12.5	17.2	19.9	16.3	30.1	17.1
Private Fixed Investment	34.9	59.8	60.7	48.8	75.8	76.5	73.6	88.4	119.5	138.9	146.2	160.6	175.3	201.7
Government Fixed Investment	27.9	40.3	55.2	59.7	51.4	73.6	85.3	74.9	72.8	64.9	94.4	103.1	113.2	120.8
Total Absorption of Goods and Services in Puerto Rico	742.0	809.5	850.0	857.3	969.5	1095.6	1143.1	1212.0	1302.2	1390.8	1505.0	1598.5	1742.8	1866.6
Plus: Sales to Rest of World	293.6	298.9	308.0	345.5	400.9	454.6	563.8	577.3	584.2	635.5	683.0	702.7	768.1	908.8
Federal Government	68.2	64.3	61.7	62.9	74.6	127.9	155.6	136.0	130.5	114.0	111.0	111.6	118.1	124.4
Other	225.4	234.6	246.3	282.6	326.2	326.7	408.2	441.3	453.7	521.6	571.9	591.1	650.0	784.4
Less: Purchases from Rest of World	419.7	441.4	440.2	452.3	553.2	578.2	656.2	707.1	761.2	831.6	938.0	989.7	1072.9	1202.9
Federal Government	20.9	16.5	13.9	16.1	14.5	21.5	28.2	28.0	26.1	22.4	19.9	21.5	23.9	26.3
Other	399.8	439.4	427.2	436.6	538.4	566.9	628.7	675.0	738.9	818.3	932.1	962.1	1058.0	1186.0
Errors and Omissions	-1.0	-14.5	-0.9	-0.4	0.2	-10.3	-0.6	4.0	-3.8	-9.0	-14.0	6.0	-9.0	-10.0
Gross Commonwealth Product	616.0	666.9	717.8	750.5	817.3	972.1	1050.7	1082.0	1125.2	1194.7	1249.9	1311.5	1438.0	1572.6
Ratio of Gross Domestic Investment to Gross Commonwealth Product	14.3%	16.1%	16.9%	14.4%	18.0%	19.8%	15.0%	16.0%	18.2%	18.5%	20.8%	21.3%	22.2%	21.6%
Annual Rate of Increase in Gross Commonwealth Product		10.8%	10.8%	4.6%	10.9%	11.9%	8.0%	3.0%	4.0%	6.2%	4.6%	4.9%	9.6%	10.9%
Per Capita Gross Product	$286	$307	$327	$341	$365	$437	$473	$491	$504	$533	$557	$578	$626	$677

[a] Detail may not add because of rounding error.

SOURCES: *Income and Product, Puerto Rico, 1959*, Commonwealth of Puerto Rico, Planning Board, n.d.; 1960 figures and some revised data supplied by Bureau of Economics and Statistics, Planning Board.

1955-1959

During the five-year period 1955-59, insular gross product continued to rise although its rate of growth declined. In the previous five-year period, insular gross product (current prices) rose 44 per cent; in the period 1955-59 it

Table 12

Summary Balance of Payments of Puerto Rico, 1955-59

(millions of dollars)

	1955	1956	1957	1958	1959
Exports of Goods and Services, total	*$558*	*$613*	*$663*	*$681*	*$744*
Merchandise and Services	454	521	572	591	650
Operational Disbursements of Federal Government	104	92	91	90	94
Imports of Goods and Services, total	*−740*	*−818*	*−932*	*−962*	*−1059*
Balance of Goods and Services	*−182*	*−205*	*−269*	*−281*	*−314*
Unilateral Transfers, net	*101*	*111*	*135*	*125*	*128*
Private	17	19	23	19	22
Federal	84	92	112	106	106
Balance of Goods, Services, and Transfers	*− 80*	*− 94*	*−134*	*−156*	*−186*
Financing (each item net):					
Puerto Rican Capital:					
Short-term	− 2	26	− 18	− 14	− 6
Long-term	− 19	− 18	7	− 6	− 17
External Capital:					
Short-term	38	12	− 1	− 15	33
Long-term (Puerto Rican Bonds)	13	6	54	58	63
Long-term (Federal Agency; Mortgage Loans, etc.)	8	9	19	38	35
Long-term Direct Investment	37	49	60	101	68
Errors	5	9	13	− 6	10

SOURCE: *Balance of Payments of Puerto Rico, 1959*, Commonwealth of Puerto Rico, Planning Board, n.d. Revised figures supplied by the Balance of Payments Section, Planning Board.

rose 24 per cent. (In constant prices, the two rates were 25 per cent and 15 per cent.) Domestic investment rose even more rapidly in this period, however, and most of the increase was in private investment. The tax-incentive program began to attract a large number of firms to the island. Thus, while federal expenditures for goods and services declined from their post-Korean peak, the rise in domestic investment and in exports far more than made up for this decline. The increases in domestic expenditures were accompanied by a sharp rise in imports, with the result that the current-account deficit rose steadily during this period.

Private direct investment now began to dominate the capital account. While bond issues of insular governments and public authorities continued to rise, they were exceeded in net amount by the inflow of capital in the form of direct investment. The pertinent facts are summarized in Table 12, a continuation of Tables 9 and 10. There it may be seen that direct external investment exceeded Puerto Rican bond issues in every year.

Also of interest is the fact that the liquidation of external short-term assets ceased in this period, and the banks began once more to accumulate such assets. The insular government continued to accumulate external long-term assets, chiefly United States bonds.

The total current-plus-U.T. deficit rose to $650 million in the five-year period, and was financed in the following manner (millions):

Method of Financing Current Account Deficits, 1955-59

Puerto Rican External Assets [acquisition (−)]		− $67
Short-term	− 14	
Long-term	− 53	
Inflow of External Capital		685
Short-term	67	
Sale of insular bonds	194	
Loans of federal agencies, mortgage loans, etc.	109	

Direct investment	315
Errors	32
Current-plus-U.T. Balance	650
Unilateral Transfers, net	600
Current-account Balance	1250

The inflow of external capital was accompanied by a vigorous expansion of insular income and product. It was also accompanied by a sharp increase in the current-account deficit. This rising deficit, far from proceeding to the point of a convertibility crisis, actually did not amount to as much as the capital inflow, thus permitting Puerto Rican banks and governments to add to their stocks of external assets.

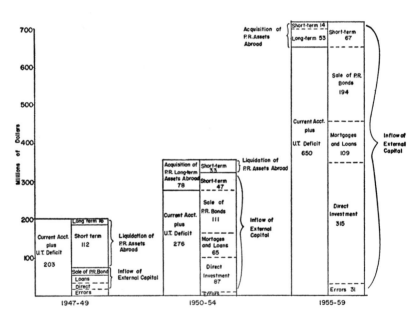

Fig. 1. Balance of Current Account Plus Unilateral Transfers, Methods of Financing.

We have arbitrarily divided the postwar span of years into three periods, basing our division upon the *chief* means used to finance the external deficit in each period. Thus we have seen that in the immediate postwar period the external deficit was financed by drawing down wartime accumulations of liquid assets; that in the period 1950-54 it was financed principally by bond issues originated by the insular government; and that the most recent period was dominated by an upsurge of private direct investment. The shifting nature of external financing is illustrated in Figure 1, which also serves to emphasize that we are describing dominant features of these periods but not sharp and exclusive categories.

Table 13

Major Sources of Federal Funds to Puerto Rico

(millions of dollars)

Fiscal Year	Operational Disbursements	Federal Transfers, Net	Excise and Customs	Total	Ratio to Total Imports	Ratio to Gross Insular Product
1946	$118	$ 23	$39	$180		
1947	47	68	23	138	33%	22%
1948	48	80	6	134	30%	20%
1949	48	71	10	129	29%	18%
1950	47	74	12	133	29%	18%
1951	60	51	17	128	23%	16%
1952	107	45	17	169	29%	17%
1953	128	51	18	197	30%	19%
1954	108	62	19	189	27%	17%
1955	104	85	21	210	28%	19%
1956	92	93	23	208	25%	17%
1957	91	117	24	232	25%	19%
1958	92	111	24	227	23%	17%
1959	105	108	21	234	22%	16%

SOURCES: *Balance of Payments of Puerto Rico, 1959*, Commonwealth of Puerto Rico, Planning Board, n.d.; *Income and Product, Puerto Rico, 1959*, Commonwealth of Puerto Rico, Planning Board, n.d.; *Statistical Yearbook of Puerto Rico, 1959*, Commonwealth of Puerto Rico, Planning Board, n.d.; and *Statistical Yearbook, Historical Statistics, 1959*, Commonwealth of Puerto Rico, Planning Board, n.d.

Table 14. *The Balance of Payments*

Item	1945	1946	1947	1948	1949
Exports of Goods and Services, total	*276.1*	*339.1*	*272.8*	*282.4*	*249.1*
Merchandise, adjusted	160.4	202.3	195.9	198.2	210.9
Transportation	7.9	10.0	15.4	17.4	15.7
Travel	1.6	3.4	4.2	5.5	6.4
Income on Investments	3.3	4.5	5.2	5.8	4.7
Operational Disbursements of Federal Agencies	102.0	117.6	47.3	47.8	47.8
Miscellaneous Services	1.1	1.4	4.8	7.7	8.6
Imports of Goods and Services, total	*222.8*	*303.4*	*399.8*	*439.4*	*427.1*
Merchandise, adjusted	185.4	260.5	327.4	367.7	355.0
Transportation	18.9	25.4	33.4	36.6	34.6
Travel	1.8	3.6	10.8	10.1	9.8
Income on Investments	11.9	8.6	17.9	12.2	14.5
Miscellaneous Services	4.8	5.3	10.3	12.8	13.2
Balance on Current Account	*53.3*	*35.7*	*-127.0*	*-157.0*	*-133.0*
Unilateral Transfers (net)	*12.1*	*25.7*	*62.6*	*77.9*	*73.2*
Private Remittances	3.3	2.3	- 5.3	- 1.9	1.8
Federal Government	8.8	23.4	*67.9*	*79.8*	*71.4*
To Commonwealth Government	—	—	5.3	6.4	8.1
To Individuals and Firms	—	—	62.6	73.4	63.3
Balance on Current Account plus Unilateral Transfers	*65.4*	*61.4*	*- 64.4*	*- 79.1*	*- 59.8*
Capital					
Puerto Rican Capital (net)	*- 95.0*	*- 43.6*	*35.4*	*46.8*	*46.3*
Short-term	- 21.6	- 32.8	55.3	24.5	32.2
Long-term	- 73.4	- 10.8	- 19.9	22.3	14.1
External Capital (net)	*22.9*	*- 16.1*	*28.0*	*17.8*	*12.7*
Short-term	15.0	- 8.7	- 1.5	12.6	- 10.2
Long-term (Puerto Rican Banks)	—	—	20.7	1.1	- 1.0
Long-term;(Fed. Agencies; Mortgages & Loans)	7.9	- 7.4	0.6	6.1	14.2
Long-term, Other Mortgages & Loans	—	—	n.a	n.a	n.a
Long-term Direct Investment	—	—	8.2	- 2.0	9.7
Errors	6.6	- 1.3	1.0	14.5	0.8
Balance on Capital Account (and Errors)	*65.4*	*61.4*	*64.4*	*79.1*	*59.8*

ᵃ Detail may not add because of rounding error.
SOURCES: R. L. Sammons and B. H. Cestero, *The Balance of External Payments of Puerto Rico, 1942-46*

of Puerto Rico[a] (millions of dollars)

1950	1951	1952	1953	1954	1955	1956	1957	1958	1959	1960
329.4	*386.4*	*433.1*	*535.6*	*549.5*	*558.1*	*613.1*	*663.0*	*681.1*	*744.2*	*882.5*
244.1	278.9	270.3	334.0	362.4	372.3	432.2	472.5	487.0	530.1	646.0
17.1	18.8	21.4	26.3	24.8	26.7	30.1	33.6	30.7	36.3	42.1
6.8	9.1	13.8	19.4	21.2	22.9	25.0	28.0	34.2	43.8	53.1
4.3	4.3	4.2	4.6	5.5	6.2	6.9	7.9	8.6	8.9	10.2
46.8	60.1	106.5	127.5	107.9	104.4	91.6	91.1	90.0	94.3	98.1
10.3	15.2	16.9	23.8	27.7	25.6	27.3	29.9	30.6	30.8	33.0
436.6	*538.4*	*566.9*	*628.6*	*675.2*	*740.0*	*818.3*	*932.0*	*962.2*	*1058.5*	*1186.4*
352.6	446.4	456.3	503.3	533.7	582.8	641.9	727.3	745.2	827.6	930.9
36.6	41.8	49.8	53.5	57.2	65.6	71.1	77.0	84.2	88.5	99.6
10.8	11.6	17.2	19.1	23.8	23.2	23.9	27.8	29.9	31.3	33.2
21.6	22.6	25.4	33.5	39.1	44.2	54.8	70.7	69.2	76.5	85.6
15.0	16.0	18.2	19.2	21.4	24.2	26.6	29.2	33.7	34.6	37.0
-107.2	*-152.0*	*-133.8*	*- 93.0*	*-125.7*	*-181.9*	*-205.0*	*-269.0*	*-281.0*	*-314.3*	*-303.9*
75.3	*59.0*	*56.3*	*67.4*	*79.0*	*101.4*	*111.2*	*134.6*	*124.5*	*128.1*	*122.1*
1.8	7.6	11.8	16.8	17.3	17.2	19.2	23.2	18.6	22.2	28.2
73.5	*51.4*	*44.5*	*50.6*	*61.7*	*84.2*	*92.0*	*111.4*	*105.9*	*106.0*	*93.9*
10.0	12.8	14.8	19.1	21.0	21.8	24.3	40.6	37.9	40.9	42.3
63.5	38.6	29.7	31.5	40.7	62.4	67.7	70.8	68.0	65.1	51.6
- 31.9	*- 93.0*	*- 77.5*	*- 25.6*	*- 46.7*	*- 80.5*	*- 94.0*	*-134.4*	*-156.6*	*-186.1*	*-181.7*
- 13.5	*1.8*	*1.0*	*- 14.7*	*- 18.0*	*- 21.1*	*8.1*	*- 10.6*	*- 20.1*	*- 23.1*	*- 7.2*
4.3	12.3	15.9	- 1.8	2.7	- 1.8	25.7	- 17.9	- 13.8	- 6.4	17.0
- 17.8	- 10.5	- 14.9	- 12.9	- 20.7	- 19.3	- 17.6	7.3	- 6.3	- 16.7	- 24.2
45.0	*91.5*	*66.2*	*40.2*	*69.9*	*96.5*	*76.7*	*131.0*	*182.6*	*199.7*	*179.1*
- 0.7	25.9	21.6	10.2	- 8.9	37.7	12.1	- 0.8	- 14.5	33.3	4.2
28.6	22.1	8.1	7.3	45.0	13.3	5.5	54.2	57.8	62.9	75.8
6.4	3.9	5.8	0.3	- 0.5	1.4	1.6	5.5	8.5	10.2	15.2
n.a	20.2	15.8	5.9	8.2	7.0	8.2	12.6	29.4	25.1	20.1
10.7	19.4	14.9	16.4	26.1	37.1	49.3	59.5	101.4	68.1	63.7
0.4	- 0.3	10.3	0.1	- 5.2	5.0	9.1	14.0	- 6.0	9.4	9.9
31.9	*93.0*	*77.5*	*25.6*	*46.7*	*80.5*	*93.9*	*134.4*	*156.6*	*186.0*	*181.7*

(Río Piedras: University of Puerto Rico, 1948), with adjustments to make their figures comparable; *Balance of Payments of Puerto Rico*, Commonwealth of Puerto Rico, Planning Board, n.d., various issues.

It may be of interest to summarize the extent to which the federal government supplied dollars to the Puerto Rican economy. Here we shall include operational disbursements, net transfer payments, and also the excise and customs taxes refunded to the Commonwealth government. The results are shown in Table 13. This table is not presented as a measure of the extent to which the Puerto Rican economy was subsidized by the federal government, nor is it a measure of the dependence of the island's economy upon federal programs. There are important omissions on both sides of the ledger that should be considered if one were trying to compute the net effect of the federal government. Nevertheless, it is of some interest to examine the size of the three largest sources of federal dollars flowing to Puerto Rico and to compare the total with insular imports and income for the postwar period.

CHAPTER V

THE PROCESS OF ADJUSTMENT IN THE BALANCE OF PAYMENTS

We have seen that in the thirteen-year period 1947 to 1959 Puerto Rico experienced a current-account deficit in her balance of payments that was financed by various forms of capital inflow. In this chapter we shall examine the process of adjustment in the balance of payments to such an inflow of capital, relating the Puerto Rican experience to theoretical explanations of this process.

In view of its historical eminence, we begin with the classical theory of transfers under gold standard conditions. In this theory, an increase in the flow of capital from A to B is expected to increase B's money supply (via an increase in gold or in bank reserves), thus increasing B's money prices and causing a rise in imports and a fall in exports. When sectoral price levels are introduced, as in Viner's Canadian study,[1] the hypothesis is that prices of B's domestic (non-traded) goods and services will rise most, prices of her exports will rise less, and import prices will rise least of all. Indeed, the prices of B's imports may even fall, since the capital-exporting country is expected to experience a decline in its domestic price level.

In the Puerto Rican case we must first attempt to define and empirically identify the pertinent statistics for "reserves" and for "money supply." The foreign-exchange reserves of the banking system may be defined to include

1. Jacob Viner, *Canada's Balance of International Payments* (Cambridge: Harvard University Press, 1923.)

all "cash items," namely coin and currency, balances with other banks (chiefly external), and cash items in process of collection.[2] Actually, only the second of these is directly analogous to the reserve concept of our theory. Holdings of currency are determined by operating needs, and cash items in process are determined by administrative and clerical routines. For the economy as a whole, foreign-exchange reserves should include currency in circulation and privately-held balances in mainland banks, but neither of these provides a basis for further expansion of the Puerto Rican money supply, and we will therefore concentrate on bank reserves.

We present in Table 15 some pertinent statistics for "all commercial banks" in Puerto Rico. There are at

Table 15
Selected Assets, All Commercial Banks

(millions of dollars)

Year (June 30)	Currency and Coin	Due from Banks	Other Cash Items	Total Cash Items	Bonds and Investments	Total Assets
1946	$25.2	$14.8	$11.6	$51.6	$156.7	$337.5
1947	27.2	15.3	7.2	49.7	141.3	317.0
1948	29.9	11.2	7.5	48.6	121.2	315.2
1949	21.6	8.8	8.8	39.4	97.9	271.4
1950	20.2	12.8	8.7	41.7	96.9	285.3
1951	25.7	12.0	10.9	48.6	87.1	320.5
1952	22.8	15.3	12.5	50.6	70.3	337.1
1953	22.7	19.9	10.8	53.4	75.5	337.1
1954	19.3	19.9	12.1	51.4	68.8	342.8
1955	22.0	16.6	14.9	53.4	78.7	360.4
1956	19.0	22.9	15.0	56.9	86.7	418.9
1957	19.3	21.8	18.2	59.3	70.6	449.1
1958	18.1	23.8	16.6	58.5	78.0	485.6
1959	21.2	22.4	18.0	61.6	95.3	553.0

SOURCE: Bureau of Bank Examinations, Department of the Treasury.

2. Cash items include domestic claims, but the bulk of them are external.

present eleven such banks, of which seven are locally chartered. It may be seen in Table 15 that commercial banks did not accumulate large amounts of reserves during the period of capital inflow, 1946 to 1959. If we treat total cash items as the relevant reserve figure, we find that the volume of reserves fell from 1946 to 1949, and then gradually rose to 1959. Half of this growth trend was imparted by the rise in items in process of collection.

One reason why the reserve balances do not behave as in the classical model is the extreme sensitivity of short-term capital. Thus, when Puerto Rican banks experience an increase in reserve balances they will immediately purchase mainland securities with newly acquired "excess reserves." Then, as they expand domestic loans, they sell mainland securities in amounts required to meet adverse clearing balances and to maintain required reserve ratios. Thus we cannot expect to find excess reserves piling up in Puerto Rican banks, later to be converted into required reserves as domestic loans and deposits are expanded. Annual data, at any rate, cannot be expected to show this sequence.

The foregoing discussion suggests that a better measure of reserves from the viewpoint of the theory under discussion would be the sum of external bank balances and holdings of short-term United States securities in banking and government sectors. This would accord with international practices. However, in Puerto Rico the matter is complicated by the fact that a large part of the bank holdings of United States securities must be held as collateral against Commonwealth government deposits. Government holdings of such securities are held in investment accounts, are largely long-term bonds, and are not in fact *used* as exchange reserves. Thus the bank and government holdings of United States securities do not exactly fit the concept of exchange reserves, although they were so used during the 1941-46 period. It may be seen in Table 15 that bank holdings of bonds and other securities, which had been built up during the war, declined steadily from 1946 to 1952. This decline resulted from the expansion of domestic loans and provided cover for adverse clearing balances with the mainland.

What really calls for explanation is the small increase in reserves, especially balances with external banks, at a time when deposit liabilities were growing so rapidly. If we deduct balances *due* to banks, the net balances due from banks are very small indeed. Yet this is the closest Puerto Rican equivalent to the "foreign exchange reserves" of a nation's banking system. A partial explanation for the modest rise in reserves is that most deposit growth occurred in time deposits, and locally-chartered banks are not required to maintain legal reserves against time deposits.[3] Furthermore, despite the small absolute amount of external balances, commercial banks have in fact held small amounts of excess reserves during this period. Perhaps the most significant aspect of this reserve question is that commercial banks can function smoothly with such small exchange reserves. Their ability to do so is largely explained by the speed and ease with which other assets can be converted into demand funds in mainland banks.

We also encounter difficulty in defining and measuring the "money supply" of Puerto Rico. The conventional definition—coin and currency outside of banks plus demand deposits—is not entirely suitable for Puerto Rico. For one thing, government deposits are relatively more important in Puerto Rico than in the United States, reflecting the larger role of government and the absence of an independent treasury. A large part of government funds are kept in time deposits, but there is no real restriction on the use of these deposits. (However, turnover in these deposits is low.) For another thing, emphasis by

---

3. Branches of U.S. banks have no legal reserve requirements under existing law, for either demand or time deposits, but they voluntarily follow the practice of maintaining a 20 per cent reserve against demand liabilities, the same as locally-chartered banks are required to keep. Canadian branches are subject to Commonwealth requirements on local banks.

commercial banks on competition for private time deposits has affected the "normal" relationship between demand and time deposits. Third, the elimination of exchange charges in 1957 affected the rate of growth in demand deposits. In a sense we should include figures for mainland deposits of Puerto Rican firms and individuals, since many deposits were held in mainland banks instead of in local banks because of the exchange charges, especially before 1957. The effective money holdings of Puerto Rican residents thus included these external balances.[4] Since 1957 the use of such balances is said to have declined because of the removal of the exchange charge formerly levied by local banks on checks received from the mainland for payment.

Alternatively, we could define the money supply to include currency plus total deposits of commercial banks. This definition would introduce some upward bias, at least in comparison with the United States, because commercial banks in Puerto Rico hold a larger share of total saving deposits than do mainland commercial banks. Other financial institutions are much less developed in Puerto Rico.

Aside from the conceptual problem of defining the money supply, we face empirical difficulties because of

4. Statistics on the amounts of mainland balances held by Puerto Rican firms and individuals are understandably difficult to come by. The Balance-of-Payments Section of the Planning Board has collected data from a partial list of firms with mainland balances. While incomplete, these date are thought to represent the bulk of such balances. I am indebted to Mr. Alberto Morales for these figures, which are in millions of dollars.

MAINLAND BANK DEPOSITS

Year	Domestic Firms	Branches and Subsidiaries of External Firms	Total
1953	$0.5	$3.6	$4.1
1954	.8	3.8	4.6
1955	2.7	8.5	11.2
1956	1.0	9.3	10.3
1957	.6	7.8	8.4
1958	.6	9.1	9.7
1959	.6	10.4	11.0

inability to measure the coin and currency component. Circulating coin and currency are relatively more important than in the United States, but no reliable estimates exist of the actual amounts. The greater importance of coin and currency is evident from even casual observation. Charge accounts are little used, and people do not often write checks to pay for retail purchases. Firms that deliver merchandise, such as milk delivery, customarily collect daily. Few firms even pay wages by check. Indeed, a law passed in an earlier period to prevent malpractices by sugar companies requires that wages be paid in cash.

In the absence of direct estimates of coin and currency outside of banks, we may obtain rough estimates by relating this measure to other, known, economic quantities. For example, we can assume that the total of currency plus demand deposits bears the same relation to gross product in Puerto Rico as in the United States. The results of calculations based upon this assumption are shown in Table 16, where it can be seen that the currency component turns out to be a much larger part of the money supply than in the United States. It is interesting to note that the proportion of currency, on this calculation, has been falling in recent years. For purposes of comparison, a similar computation is made for a money supply defined to include time deposits.

Of course the key assumption in these calculations is that income velocity of money in Puerto Rico is the same as in the United States. Such an assumption is hard to defend, but it is difficult to find a more defensible one. Because of the variability of income velocity among nations,[5] as well as through time, we have no firm basis for choosing one level rather than another, and the money supply estimates must be regarded as rough guesses. It is

5. Cf. Ernest Doblin, "The Ratio of Income to Money Supply: An International Survey," *Review of Economics and Statistics*, 33 (August, 1951), 201-13; and Milton Friedman, "The Demand for Money: Some Theoretical and Empirical Results," *Journal of Political Economy*, 67 (August, 1959), 327-51.

worthy of note, however, that the estimates in Table 16, A, indicate that the amount of currency in circulation was about the same in 1960 as in 1947. This result is consistent with our estimate of Chapter II, namely that *net* currency movements were zero. One implication of this result is that the share of currency in the money supply has declined from nearly 50 per cent in 1947 to about 32 per cent in 1960. This is certainly the direction of change we would expect.

These empirical problems make it difficult for us to relate the capital inflow to changes in the money supply. Except for the postwar years when accumulated demand was being worked off, the money supply has increased; but

Table 16

Estimates of the Supply of Money in Puerto Rico

(millions of dollars)

A. Supply of Money defined to include Currency and Demand Deposits

Year (June 30)	GNP	Factor[a]	Estimated Supply of Money (D.D. plus Curr.)	Actual Demand Deposits (June 30)	Estimate of Currency in Circulation	Estimate of Change in Currency
1947	616	.48	296	153	143	—
1948	667	.42	280	152	128	−15
1949	718	.42	302	140	162	+34
1950	751	.39	293	141	152	−10
1951	817	.35	289	173	116	−36
1952	972	.35	340	172	168	+52
1953	1050	.35	368	174	194	+26
1954	1082	.35	380	178	202	+ 8
1955	1125	.33	375	192	183	−19
1956	1195	.32	382	216	166	−17
1957	1250	.30	375	236	139	−27
1958	1312	.30	394	234	160	+21
1959	1438	.30	441	251	190	+30
1960	1573	.28	440	300	140	−50

(Table 16 continued)

B. Supply of Money Defined to Include Currency, Demand and Time Deposits

Year (June 30)	Factor[b]	Estimated Supply of Money (All deposits plus currency)	Actual Total Deposits (June 30)	Estimate of Currency	Estimate of Change in Currency
1947	.70	431	274	157	—
1948	.64	427	277	150	− 7
1949	.64	460	250	210	+60
1950	.60	451	270	181	−29
1951	.53	433	292	141	−40
1952	.53	515	293	222	+81
1953	.53	557	301	256	+34
1954	.55	595	301	294	+38
1955	.52	585	323	262	−32
1956	.51	609	357	252	−10
1957	.50	625	404	221	−31
1958	.52	682	446	236	+15
1959	.50	719	508	211	−25
1960	.48	755	562	193	−18

[a] This factor is the United States ratio of money supply to GNP, where the money supply is defined as demand deposits plus currency outside banks.

[b] This factor is the United States ratio of money supply to GNP, where money supply includes *time* deposits.

SOURCES: *Federal Reserve Bulletin*, for U.S. ratios of money supply to GNP; Bureau of Banks Examinations, Department of the Treasury, for Puerto Rican demand and time deposits.

it has not increased steadily, and changes in the money supply are not related in a clearcut fashion to the inflows of capital. In Table 17, we show the net movements of external long-term capital along with our series for deposits and our money supply estimates. It is clear from these figures that capital inflow has not set in motion a multiple expansion of the money supply, as contemplated in theory. One explanation of this was given in Chapter IV, where it was shown that capital inflows are quickly followed (accompanied) by increases in imports, with only small changes occurring in bank reserves and the money supply. It may be that postwar expansion in the Puerto Rican money supply is not so much associated with the short-run monetary effects of capital inflow as it is the result of the increase in productive capacity as investment projects are completed and begin operations. The operation of new productive capacity generates increases in exports, and proceeds of export sales may "stick" in added reserves and in expanded deposits to a greater extent than do the proceeds of new capital inflow.

Although movements of reserves and money supply do not correspond to those contemplated in the theory, available price-level indices display movements that are roughly consistent with the hypothesis stated above. The composite consumers' price index for wage earners' families (1947-49 = 100) stood at 101.8 in June 1947. By June, 1958, it had risen to 121.8, an increase of 20 per cent.

Table 17

Capital Inflow and Changes in the Money Supply

(millions of dollars)

Year	Net Inflow of Long-term External Capital	Change in Estimated Money Supply	Change in Demand Deposits	Change in Total Deposits
1947	29	n.a	−25	−33
1948	5	−16	− 1	3
1949	23	22	−12	−27
1950	46	−17	1	20
1951	66	9	32	22
1952	45	56	− 1	1
1953	30	28	2	8
1954	79	12	4	0
1955	59	65	14	22
1956	65	7	24	34
1957	132	− 7	20	47
1958	197	19	− 2	42
1959	166	47	17	62
1960	175	31	49	54

SOURCES: Table 14 and Table 16.

As noted above, the modified classical theory yields a prediction of different price changes for domestic goods, exports, and imports. Unfortunately, the Puerto Rican consumer price index cannot easily be subdivided in this way. Only for food products is there a clear-cut distinction between locally produced and imported items. In this case the price patterns are consistent with expectations—the price index for locally produced food rose from 101.2 in 1947 to 151.6 in 1958, while that for imported food rose only from 102.6 to 103.6.

Other components in the consumers' price index are grouped in Table 18 according to whether they are "chiefly" produced domestically or imported. For each component we show the percentage price change from 1947 to 1958. According to our hypothesis, we expect the prices of domestic products to rise more than do the prices of imported products. A glance at Table 18 shows that this expectation is realized. *Every* category of domestic goods and services rose more in price than did *any* category of imported goods.

Another bit of evidence to support this interpretation of the price effect is provided by terms-of-trade calculations made for the period 1947 to 1958. The export-price index rose from 100.0 in 1947 to 115.8 in 1958, while the import-price index rose from 100.5 to 105.9. Thus the terms of trade changed in Puerto Rico's favor by about 10 per cent from 1947 to 1958.[6] It also seems highly probable that domestic non-traded goods and services rose by considerably more than 10 per cent during the same period. Thus the price increase was greatest for domestic goods, followed by exports and then imports, which is the ranking one would expect on the basis of theory.

This consistency of experience with theoretical expectations should not be taken too seriously, however. It may be that Puerto Rican prices have simply followed the

6. $115.8/100.0 \div 105.9/100.5 = 109.9$. Figures supplied by Balance-of-Payments Section, Planning Board.

Table 18

Consumer Price Indexes (1947-49 = 100)

	June 1947	June 1958	Percentage Change 6/47-6/58
"Chiefly" Domestic Goods and Services:			
Locally Produced Food	101.2	151.6	+50%
Rent	98.0	127.7	+29%
Light and Fuel	98.6	123.1	+25%
Furniture	103.5	123.1	+19%
Medical Care	99.2	118.2	+19%
Personal Care	99.7	151.1	+52%
Education and Recreation	96.7	123.4	+28%
Tobacco, Rum and Beer	100.4	132.5	+32%
Transportation	100.1	116.5	+16%
"Chiefly" Imported Goods and Services:			
Imported Food	102.6	103.6	+ 1%
Textile and Plastics	105.1	102.2	− 3%
Kitchen Equipment	103.9	112.0	+ 8%
Clothing and Related Items	105.8	103.9	− 2%
Other Housefurnishings	104.4	112.7	+ 8%
Household	104.1	97.3	− 7%

SOURCE: *Statistical Yearbook of Puerto Rico, 1959*, Commonwealth of Puerto Rico, Planning Board, n.d.

pattern of United States prices. It is well-known that prices of personal services, medical care, and education have risen more than prices of staple foods, textile products, and clothing. "Locally produced" foodstuffs in Puerto Rico mean chiefly fruits and fresh vegetable, and prices of these products have also risen sharply in the United States. Furthermore, in the Puerto Rican economy the prices of these products are largely dependent on the price of personal services of the growers, which tend to follow other kinds of service wages. This suggestion is strengthened by comparing the following percentage price changes for components of the United States consumer price index with those for Puerto Rico:[7]

Group	Percentage change, June, 1947- June, 1958	
	U.S. Prices	P.R. Prices
Food	23%	50%
Rent	47%	29%
Medical Care	51%	19%
Personal Care	32%	52%
Apparel	10%	−2%
Reading and Recreation	22%	28%

Despite this word of caution, Puerto Rican experience nevertheless suggests that even within the United States common-market area the classical price effect plays a part in the process of adjustment to interregional capital movements.

Next we wish to see how well the modern theory of income effects fits Puerto Rican experience. These two explanations, classical and modern, are sometimes opposed to each other in the literature, as if one must choose between them. That is not our purpose here, since it seems more appropriate to treat them as supplementary explanations or as alternative theoretical constructs. Indeed, it may be that the price effect is most fully in operation when *no* price changes occur. For example, if foreign supply is perfectly elastic, and if consumers will readily substitute imported for domestic goods, then with a rise in total expenditures the slightest increase in domestic prices will lead to increased imports. This case is usually treated as an income effect, but it is the extreme sensitivity to price changes that accounts for the quick rise in imports in such circumstances. In the limiting case, where 100 per cent of the increase in expenditures is directed toward imports, the actual increase in income is minimized even though no changes in sectoral prices occur. On the other hand, where

7. U.S. prices are from *Federal Reserve Bulletin*.

enough expenditures are directed toward home goods to drive up their prices relative to imports, the rise in domestic incomes, and therefore the income effect on imports, will be greater than before even though sectoral price changes now appear to be consistent with the classical price effects.

According to income theory, capital inflows to finance an expansion of domestic investment are accompanied by increases in expenditures that lead in turn, via the multiplier, to increases in income and in other expenditures. Imports increase as part of the increment of income is spent for imports; the current account turns passive; and the "real transfer" is accomplished.[8] Most statements of this process are concerned with short-run monetary adjustment, and the quantities of capital and other resources are assumed to be constant. In the Puerto Rican case, where the stock of capital is growing rapidly, it is necessary to allow for the capacity effect in order to account properly for the growth in exports and income.[9]

In the broadest sense, the aggregate inflow of capital is measured by the current-account deficit. This deficit represents the extent to which the economy draws goods and services from the external world in excess of its supplies of goods and services to the external world, or it represents the excess of "absorption" over production. We have seen in Chapter IV the various ways in which this deficit is financed in Puerto Rico. Since 1950 a large part of it has been financed by long-term capital inflows.

It is clear that Puerto Rico's high level of domestic investment has been made possible by the capital inflow. We show in Table 19 some series for current-account

8. As before we omit "foreign repercussions" arising from the fact that increased imports represent increased exports for the U.S.; and will thus increase income there. The effect of such an increase of U.S. income upon Puerto Rican exports is so small as to be ignored in the following discussion. (This is not to say that changes in the level of U.S. income have no effect on Puerto Rican exports.)

9. Cf. J. C. Ingram, "Growth in Capacity and Canada's Balance of Payments," *American Economic Review*, 47 (March, 1957), 93-104.

Table 19

Measures of Gross Capital Inflow and Domestic Investment

(millions of dollars)

Year	Current Account Balance	Gross Domestic Investment	Balance on Current Account plus Unilateral Transfers	Long-term Capital (external), net
1947	−127.0	88.0	− 64.4	29.5
1948	−157.0	107.4	− 79.1	5.2
1949	−133.0	121.6	− 59.8	22.9
1950	−107.2	107.8	− 31.9	45.7
1951	−152.0	146.9	− 93.0	65.6
1952	−133.8	192.6	− 77.5	44.6
1953	− 93.0	157.5	− 25.6	30.0
1954	−125.7	172.7	− 46.7	78.8
1955	−181.9	204.8	− 79.3	58.9
1956	−205.2	221.0	− 92.8	64.7
1957	−269.0	260.5	−129.2	131.8
1958	−281.0	280.0	−156.6	197.2
1959	−314.3	318.6	−186.1	166.4
1960	−303.9	339.6	−181.7	174.9

SOURCE: *Balance of Payment of Puerto Rico, 1959*, Commonwealth of Puerto Rico, Planning Board, n.d. Revisions and 1960 estimates supplied by the Balance-of-Payments Section of the Planning Board.

deficit, inflow of external long-term capital, and gross domestic investment. It can be seen in this table that (1) since the immediate post-war years, when consumption was catching up, the current-account deficit closely parallels gross domestic investment, and (2) since 1950 an increasing share of gross investment has been financed by long-term capital inflows.

In order to develop an income model for Puerto Rican experience, it is first necessary to make some estimates of the pertinent marginal propensities. As usually stated, the key parameters of the model are the marginal propensity to consume domestic goods, the marginal propensity to consume imports, and the marginal propensity to save. Ordinarily, it is implicitly assumed that domestic investment does not include an imported component. When changes in domestic investment are being treated as the autonomous variable, it is usually assumed that no changes in exports are involved in the process of adjustment to a given disturbance. One reason for this assumption is that the analysis concerns only the short-run monetary effects of domestic investment and does not consider the effects of operation of the new capital facilities.

Even where increases in exports are allowed for, as in Metzler's interregional model, the usual assumption is that exports do not contain imported merchandise. For example, in Metzler's model the following matrix of expenditures is presented:[10]

Expenditures / Receipts	Region 1	Region 2	Total Income
Region 1	E_{11}	M_{21}	$E_{11} + M_{21} =$ Income of Region 1
Region 2	M_{12}	E_{22}	$E_{22} + M_{12} =$ Income of Region 2
Total Expenditures:	$E_{11} + M_{12}$	$E_{22} + M_{21}$	

The first subscript denotes the region making the expenditure, the second subscript denotes the region in which it is made. Thus M_{12} represents the expenditures of Region 1 in Region 2—that is, Region 1's imports from Region 2. Similarly, M_{21} represents Region 1's exports to Region 2. The income of Region 1 is then equal to $E_{11} + M_{21}$—that is, its own expenditures for domestic product plus its exports to Region 2. The marginal propensity to import can be

10. L. A. Metzler, "A Multiple-Region Theory of Income and Trade," *Econometrica*, 18 (1950), 329-54.

calculated by relating total import to income or the ratio $[M_{12}/(E_{11}+M_{21})]$. But this assumes that none of the imports are re-exported. It assumes that M_{21} measures external expenditures on Region 1's domestic resources but that none of the value of M_{21} was originally imported by Region 1. While this treatment is admissible in theoretical statements, it makes difficult the use of reported statistics of income and trade for empirical analysis. It often happens, for example, that in the fraction $[M_{12}/E_{11}+M_{21}]$ Region 1's exports include a large imported component, and therefore the reported statistics for M_{12} and M_{21} contain a common element that should be eliminated in order to compute the empirical equivalent of the marginal propensity to import. (In the denominator this is usually taken care of, since gross product or income is calculated by deducting gross imports from total net product for C, I, and X. It is the numerator that causes the trouble.)[11]

Because Puerto Rican exports include an important import component, it is necessary to allow for this in estimating the parameters. We begin by dividing total imports into three categories: imports for consumption, investment, and export. That is, we wish to calculate:

$$C_t = C_d + C_m$$
$$I_t = I_d + I_m$$
$$X_t = X_d + X_m,$$

where: $M_t = C_m + I_m + X_m$.

The above symbols are used as follows: C for consumption, I for investment, X for exports, M for imports, Y for gross insular product.

The subscripts are used as follows: d for domestic, m for imports, t for total.

It should be noted that government expenditures are divided into "consumption" and "investment" components and are therefore not shown separately.

It follows that:

11. Cf. J. E. Meade, *The Balance of Payments* (London: Oxford Press, 1951), pp. 38-39.

$C_d + I_d + X_d =$ Gross Insular Product $= C_t + I_t + X_t - M_t$.
Published estimates of gross insular product, as in Table
11 of Chapter IV, show only the right-hand side of this
equation. In order to compute the components on the left,
it is necessary to allocate total imports into the three
categories.[12]

Puerto Rican statistics show an increasing rate of
growth in imports with respect to income that is not a
result of domestic utilization of imports. See Figure 2 for

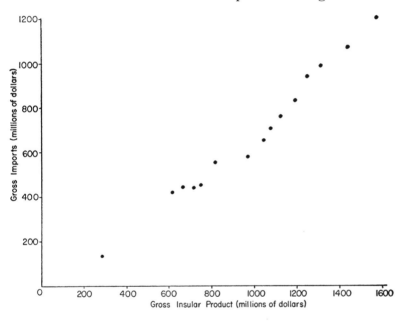

FIG. 2. Scatter Diagram: Total Imports and Gross Insular Product,
1940, 1947-60. (Source: Table 11).

12. It should be noted that we are here using "exports" and "imports" to
include the whole of the current-account items. In subsequent computations
we will in fact use the income and product concepts of purchases from, and sales
to, the rest of the world. Difficult conceptual problems arise when one tries to
furnish the economic meaning of allocating some items among consumption,
investment, and exports. Consider, for example, the "imports" item, income
on investments.

the scatter diagram of M_t and Y. In recent years the change in imports has almost equalled the change in income, and by 1960 the ratio of total imports to total insular product was about 0.75. However, a large part of these imports entered into the production of goods that were subsequently exported.

Our first problem is to derive a relationship between imports for consumption and income (C_m/Y), which we can do only by making some rough estimates. The Planning Board has estimated that for a dollar of gross fixed investment it is necessary to import 51 cents worth of materials and machinery and to pay 4 cents for transportation and other charges.[13] Thus 55 per cent of the gross fixed investment is spent for imports. We will assume that this ratio has been stable for the period 1947 to 1960.

Before 1947, merchandise exports were dominated by sugar, rum, and tobacco, the value of which did not include much imported materials. Since 1947 the Fomento program has greatly expanded the manufacturing sector, and the new exports generated from this sector are based heavily on imported raw materials. Most of the Fomento factories import parts and materials, process and assemble them in Puerto Rico, and ship the finished product back to the mainland. Thus, as the manufacturing sector has expanded and increased the exports of manufactures, imports have also risen. No detailed estimates of the import content of exports have been made, and we shall have to be satisfied with rough estimates. We will assume that 50 per cent of the export value of "new products" is made up of imported goods and services. Even though the ratio of imports is higher than 50 per cent for some industries and lower for others, we have some basis for assuming the average to be about 50 per cent. Calculations based on data of the Census of Manufacturers suggest that the "cost of materials" comprises about half the "value of

13. *Economic Report to the Governor, 1959*, Commonwealth of Puerto Rico, Planning Board, p. 30. This relationship is reported to have been steady in recent years.

shipments to the U.S." for a selected list of manufacturing industries, after excluding sugar, rum, and tobacco. Furthermore, of the total receipts of tax-exempt industries in 1954, value added by manufacture was about 50 per cent.[14] The other half of total receipts would consist primarily of materials, and these are largely imported.

We will assume in the following calculations that the import content of exports is equal to the amount of manufacturing net income in tax-exempt firms—that half their total sales receipts is made up of imported raw materials. This is obviously a rough estimate, and there is some evidence that the percentage is rising above 50 per cent in

Table 20

Calculation of $C_d + C_m$, $X_d + X_m$

(millions of dollars)

Fiscal Year	$I_m = .55 I_t$	X_m[a]	$C_m = M_t - (I_m + X_m)$	$C_d = C_t - C_m$	Retained Imports $(C_m + I_m)$
1947	48	25	347	307	395
1948	59	26	356	346	415
1949	67	27	346	382	413
1950	59	29	364	386	423
1951	81	33	439	384	520
1952	106	37	435	468	541
1953	87	54	515	471	602
1954	95	82	530	509	625
1955	113	93	555	542	668
1956	122	115	595	575	717
1957	144	130	664	581	808
1958	154	139	697	622	851
1959	175	162	736	688	911
1960	187	196	820	707	1007

[a] Re-exports assumed to be twenty-five in 1947 before tax-exempt program was started. This is a rough estimate based upon the composition of merchandise exports in that year. For remaining years, it is assumed that tax-exempt firms purchased imported raw materials and processed them for export in an amount equal to the manufacturing net income of these firms. Or, in other words it is assumed that the output of these firms was *exported* and that the output was composed of 50 per cent imports in value.

14. *Statistical Yearbook, Historical Statistics, 1959*, Commonwealth of Puerto Rico, Planning Board, p. 105.

recent years, but it will have to suffice. We also estimate that in 1947 exports included $25 million of imports. This is based upon examination of the commodity composition of exports in that year. Needlework exports was the only commodity group that would have contained much imported materials.

The calculations based upon these assumptions are given in Table 20. There we estimate I_m, C_m, and X_m, and this enables us to calculate a series for C_d. On the basis of these estimates, we will estimate the marginal propensities required in the income model.

Figure 3 shows the relationship between total consump-

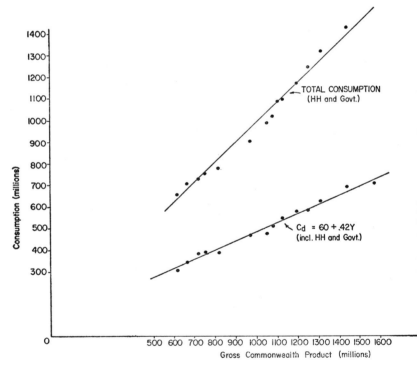

Fig. 3. Propensity to Consume, Scatter Diagram, 1947-60.
(Source: Tables 11 and 20).

tion (of both households and government)[15] and gross insular product. Using the estimates of imports for consumption made in Table 20, we can also plot the relationship between total consumption of domestic goods and services and the gross insular product. This is also shown in Figure 3, where the straight-line consumption function indicates a marginal propensity to consume domestic goods (c_d) of 0.42.[16]

In Figure 4 we show the relationship between imports for consumption and gross insular product. The marginal propensity to import consumption goods (c_m) is estimated to be 0.49. The sum of these two is $c_d + c_m = 0.91$. Thus the marginal propensity to save is: $s = 1.00 - .91 = 0.09$.

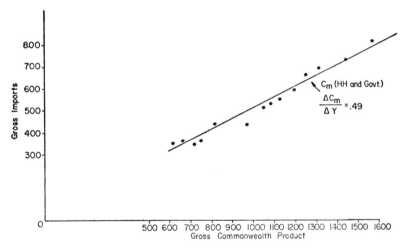

Fig. 4. Propensity to Import (for Consumption), Scatter Diagram, 1947-60. (Source: Table 20).

15. Insular income and product estimates separate Commonwealth government expenditures into consumption and investment outlays. To simplify this analysis we will use the total consumption and investment figures, thus lumping the public and private sectors together.

16. This coefficient and others to be discussed below were estimated by least-squares regression. In all cases the simple correlation coefficient was large (.98 or better), and "r" was significant at the 0.01 level, using the F-test. I am indebted to Stephen Hu for these calculations.

Using these estimates for the marginal propensities, we can illustrate the monetary effect of a given increase in capital inflow for the purpose of financing an increase in domestic investment. Let us assume that the additional capital inflow is $100 million. Then we have (all capital letters refer to changes in the variables):

$$I_t = I_d + I_m$$
$$I_m = .55I_t = 55$$
$$I_d = 45$$
$$Y = 45\left(\frac{1}{s+c_m}\right) = 45\left(\frac{1}{.09+.49}\right) = 45(1.7) = 78$$
$$C_d = .42Y = 33$$
$$C_m = .49Y = 38$$
$$C_t = C_d + C_m = 33 + 38 = 71$$
$$S = 78 - 71 = 7$$
$$M_t = I_m + C_m = 55 + 38 = 93.$$

The capital inflow is thus accompanied by increased imports of ninety-three, and the real transfer of capital is almost complete. The balance-of-payments effect of this transaction is as follows:

Balance of Payments

Dr.		Cr.
Imports	93	
S-T Assets	7	L-T Capital 100

Puerto Rican banks are left with an additional $7 million of mainland deposits or short-term securities that will enable them to expand domestic loans by a small amount, as we saw in the previous chapter.

It is worthy of note that the investment multiplier is only 0.78, if we use gross domestic investment as the multiplicand ($\Delta Y / \Delta I = 78/100 = .78$). Imports in fact rise more than domestic income because of the high import content of gross investment. This is one reason for the large increases in imports in relation to income in Puerto Rican postwar experience. A further reason is the rising import content of exports, already referred to.

We have seen that Puerto Rican marginal propensities to spend are such as to cause an increase in investment to bring about a quick increase in imports and to limit the increase in money income. Larger multiple increases in income do not occur because of the highly sensitive response in imports, as expressed in the marginal propensities, and because such a large part of the initial investment outlay is made for imports.

This analysis helps us to explain postwar experience in Puerto Rico, but it is not a complete explanation because the capacity effects are omitted, and consequently the upsurge of exports is not taken into account. The trouble is that the theory we have utilized so far is designed to portray the consequences of a given increase in autonomous expenditures but not to reflect changes in economic structure and resources such as have accompanied Puerto Rico's rapid development. One way to use this theory in connection with the Puerto Rican case would be simply to include changes in exports along with changes in investment as an autonomous expenditure and then to trace the income effects of changes in both categories of expenditure. Some calculations of this sort are shown in Table 21 as Case I. We treat the domestic component of exports (X_d) as part of the multiplicand. We can then use the same formula as before:

$$Y = (I_d + X_d) \left(\frac{1}{s + c_m}\right) = (I_d + X_d) \left(\frac{1.00}{.09 + .49}\right).$$

The total change in exports is $X_t = X_d + X_m$, and this must be taken as an autonomous variable. The total change in imports is $M_t = C_m + I_m + X_m$, where I_m and X_m are calculated as before, and $C_m = .49Y$.

Using these relationships, and given the values for I and X in each period, we can generate a series for income and imports to project a current-account balance. These calculations are given in Table 21, and the results are compared with actual figures in Figure 5. The cumulative series perform fairly well, but the first differences exhibit

Table 21

Case I: Conventional Multiplier Calculations Using $(\Delta I_d + \Delta X_d)$ as the Multiplicand

Year	ΔI_d[a]	ΔX_d[b]	$(\Delta I_d + \Delta X_c)$	$\Delta Y^c = (\Delta I_d + \Delta X_d)\left(\dfrac{1}{s+c_m}\right)$	Projected Y_t (cumul.)	$\Delta C_m = (c_m \cdot \Delta Y)$
1947	—	—	—	—	616	—
1948	8	4	12	20	636	10
1949	7	8	15	26	652	13
1950	−6	36	30	51	703	25
1951	17	51	68	116	819	57
1952	21	50	71	121	940	59
1953	−16	92	76	130	1070	64
1954	7	−15	−8	−14	1056	−7
1955	14	−4	10	17	1073	8
1956	7	30	37	63	1136	32
1957	18	32	50	85	1221	43
1958	9	11	20	34	1255	17
1959	18	42	60	100	1355	49
1960	9	107	116	197	1552	97

Year	Projected ΔM_t $(=\Delta I_m + \Delta X_m + \Delta C_m)$	Projected M_t (cumul.)	Projected Current Account (actual X_t −projected M_t)
1947		(420)	(−136)
1948	22	442	−143
1949	22	464	−156
1950	19	483	−137
1951	83	566	−165
1952	88	654	−209
1953	62	716	−152
1954	29	745	−168
1955	37	782	−198
1956	63	845	−209
1957	80	925	−242
1958	36	961	−258
1959	93	1054	−286
1960	143	1197	−288

[a] $\Delta I_d = 45\%$ of changes in Gross Domestic Investment.
[b] ΔX_d calculated from Table 16.
[c] Values given in text are used for: $cs = .09, m = .49$.

large discrepancies between projected and actual figures. These discrepancies are, of course, to be expected since we are using constant marginal propensities for the entire period.

This formulation enables us to "explain," or account for, the behavior of Puerto Rican income, imports, and current-account balance in the period 1947 to 1960. Given the estimates of marginal propensities, and given the amounts of investment and exports, the model accounts fairly well for cumulative changes in income and imports. However, it may be objected that too much information is required in this model. Gross investment and exports represent about two-thirds of the gross insular product in this period, leaving only one-third to be explained. Against this objection it may be noted that our model does explain quite well the behavior of imports and the current-account balance, which was its primary purpose. Another objection is that, especially for income, the differences in year-to-year changes between actual and projected figures are quite large. These discrepancies are concealed in the cumulative figures plotted in Figure 5 but they may be seen by comparing actual and projected year-to-year changes. The model performs somewhat better for imports than for income, however.

In order to overcome part of the first objection, above, we may utilize another method of approach, as in Case II. We can introduce changes in capacity and thus derive the changes in exports instead of taking them as given magnitudes. Annual investment outlays represent changes in the resource base and capacity to produce of the economy. Changes in the labor force have the same effect, although in Puerto Rico the labor force has not increased as much as might be expected, because of emigration. The employed population has remained fairly stable, although a shift from agricultural to non-agricultural employment has occurred. We will therefore concentrate on the relation between increments in output and in capital. Assuming

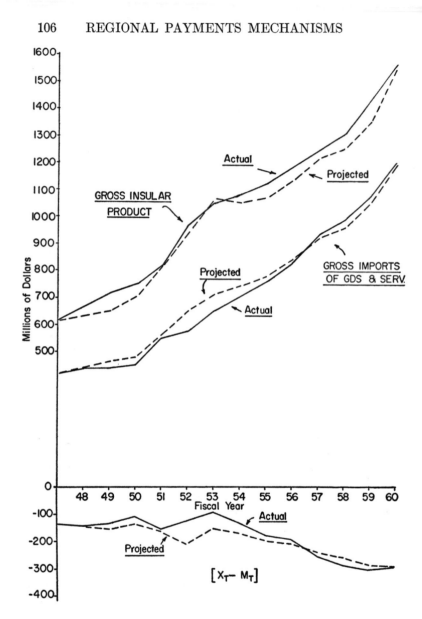

Fig. 5. Model Projections of Gross Product and Imports: Case I.
(Source: Tables 11 and 21).

Table 22
Output-Capital Ratios
(current dollars)

Year	Y	ΔY	I (Gross)	$\dfrac{\Delta Y}{I(t-1)}$ (Output/capital ratio)
1947	616	329	88	—
1948	667	51	107	.58
1949	718	51	122	.48
1950	751	33	108	.27
1951	817	66	147	.61
1952	972	55	193	.37
1953	1050	78	158	.40
1954	1082	32	173	.20
1955	1125	43	205	.25
1956	1195	70	221	.29
1957	1250	55	261	.25
1958	1312	62	280	.24
1959	1438	126	319	.45
1960	1573	135	340	.42

Year	Gross Fixed I	$\dfrac{\Delta Y}{\text{Gross Fixed } I\,(t-1)}$	Net I	$\dfrac{\Delta Y}{\text{Net } I\,(t-1)}$
1947	63	—	65	—
1948	100	.81	81	.78
1949	116	.51	90	.63
1950	109	.29	71	.37
1951	127	.60	105	.93
1952	150	.43	147	.52
1953	159	.52	107	.53
1954	163	.21	116	.30
1955	192	.26	140	.37
1956	204	.36	149	.50
1957	241	.27	180	.37
1958	264	.26	188	.34
1959	289	.47	216	.67
1960	323	.46	225	.63

SOURCE: Table 11.

that investment projects in a given year come into fruition in the next (a one-year gestation period), and also assuming that increments to capacity are fully utilized, the actual data show a considerable variation in the incremental output-capital ratio. This variation exists whether we use gross investment or net investment, gross fixed investment or net fixed investment, constant prices or current prices. Table 22 contains some of these series. The average incremental output capital ratio for the period 1947 to 1960 is 0.44, using gross fixed investment and current dollars. The ratio appears to be distinctly higher in the period 1947 through 1953 than in the period 1954 to 1960. This is puzzling, since public investment in heavily capital-intensive projects was relatively more important in the earlier period, and it might have been expected that the output-capital ratio would be higher for manufacturing, which has been more important in the later period, than for the public investments of the earlier one.

Be that as it may, the annual increase in gross insular product averaged 44 per cent of the previous year's gross fixed investment for the period 1947-60. The increments in output were partly used domestically for consumption (C_d) and investment (I_d); the remainder became available for export (X_d). The amount used for consumption depends upon the marginal propensity to consume domestic goods and services, $c_d = \Delta C_d / \Delta Y$. The remainder, $(s + c_m) \Delta Y$, is available for investment or export. If we calculate $(s + c_m) \Delta Y$, we can then deduct ΔI_d and obtain the value of ΔX_d.

By making use of the marginal propensities described above, and assuming a fixed output-capital ratio, we can generate series for Y and for X, M, and the current account of the balance of payments. These computations for Case II are shown in Table 23, and the resulting series for Y, X, M, and the current-account balance are depicted in Figure 6.

This approach yields a better fit for imports, but a

Table 23

Case II: Model Projections of Imports and Exports

Year	Gross Fixed Investment	ΔI	ΔY $(=I_{t-1}\cdot\sigma)^a$	ΔM_c $(=.49$ $\Delta Y)$	ΔM_I $(=.55$ $\Delta I)$	ΔM_x (See Table 20)	ΔM_t
1947	63	—	—	—	—	—	—
1948	100	37	28	14	20	1	35
1949	116	16	44	22	9	1	32
1950	109	−7	51	25	−4	2	23
1951	127	18	48	24	10	4	38
1952	150	23	56	27	13	4	44
1953	159	9	66	32	5	17	54
1954	163	4	70	34	2	28	64
1955	192	29	72	35	16	11	62
1956	204	12	84	41	7	22	70
1957	241	37	90	44	20	15	79
1958	264	23	106	52	13	9	74
1959	289	25	116	57	14	23	94
1960	323	34	127	62	19	34	115

Year	ΔX_d $[=(s+c_m)\Delta Y -\Delta I_d]$	ΔX_m $(=\Delta M_x,$ above)	ΔX_t	CUMULATIVE PROJECTIONS			
				Y	X_t	M_t	(X_t-M_t)
1947	—	—	—	616	294	420	−126
1948	−1	1	0	644	294	455	−161
1949	17	1	18	688	312	487	−175
1950	33	2	35	739	347	510	−163
1951	20	4	24	787	371	548	−177
1952	22	4	26	843	397	592	−195
1953	34	17	51	909	448	646	−198
1954	39	28	67	979	515	710	−195
1955	29	11	40	1051	555	772	−217
1956	44	22	66	1135	621	842	−221
1957	35	15	50	1225	671	921	−250
1958	51	9	60	1331	731	995	−264
1959	56	23	79	1447	810	1089	−279
1960	59	34	93	1574	903	1204	−301

a σ=output/capital ratio=.44.

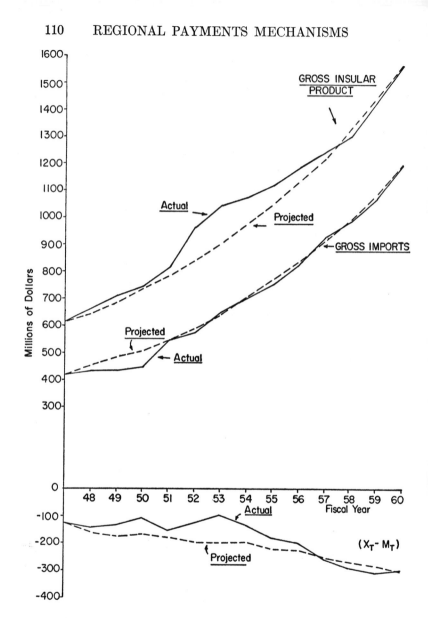

Fig. 6. Model Projections of Gross Product and Imports: Case II.
(Source: Tables 11 and 23).

poorer one for gross product and current-account balance, than did the previous one. However, it should be emphasized that we are here taking only the amount of gross fixed investment as given and then calculating values for the other variables with the aid of our computed values for the marginal propensities and output-capital ratio. This approach thus yields a projection for exports, while the previous approach was based on *given* values for exports.

On the whole, adjustments in the Puerto Rican balance of payments are explained very well by income analysis, especially when growth in capacity is allowed for. It is true that the analysis is oversimplified by the use of constant marginal propensities, but the pattern of response to the heavy capital inflow since 1946 is made clear. The low values found for the investment multiplier and for expansion of the money supply are counterparts of the fact that Puerto Rico is tightly integrated with the United States economy.

Conceptual similarities between international and interregional trade have long been recognized, but in most countries statistics are not available for interregional balance-of-payments analysis.[17] Our results support the accepted view that interregional trade differs only in degree from international trade. This view may be especially valid under the unit banking system of the United States, since the analogy between that system and the banking systems of separate nations is extremely close. One of the key aspects of the difference in degree concerns the extent to which the capital markets are integrated. Financial institutions in Puerto Rico can and do shift readily between insular financial claims and United States claims, as the situation warrants. This easy shift from "domestic" to "external" claims is sharply different in degree from the practices of financial institutions in differ-

17. Some of the studies attempted for U.S. regions are described in Walter Isard *et al.*, *Methods of Regional Analysis* (New York: Technology Press and John Wiley, 1960), Chapter 5.

ent nations, and it accounts in large part for the smooth short-run adjustments in Puerto Rico's external accounts.

As we have noted above, the roles of price effects and income effects in balance-of-payments adjustment are difficult to separate conceptually. Our results yield no preference for either approach from a theoretical viewpoint. But for empirical purposes, income analysis is definitely superior in the Puerto Rican case. We were unable even to obtain reliable estimates of the money supply in Puerto Rico, and a clear empirical definition of "foreign exchange reserves" proved difficult. Indeed, it seems clear that the money supply in Puerto Rico is an outcome, a result, of economic processes, rather than a variable subject to deliberate control by policy makers. In the determination of economic policy in the Commonwealth government, the money supply is rarely ever mentioned. This omission is partly a reflection of the fact that Puerto Rico is regarded as a region of the United States, and monetary policy is determined at the national level. In another sense the Commonwealth government is actually influencing the money supply when it fixes the levels of spending, taxing, and borrowing. Decisions regarding these matters are made by Puerto Rican authorities within certain limits—limits which are partly determined externally. However, the limits to Puerto Rican decisions are also determined in part by circumstances and considerations functionally equivalent to those which influence monetary policy in separate nations. In making its decisions about matters that partake of the nature of monetary policy, the Puerto Rican authorities find it more convenient and meaningful to discuss the issues in terms of fiscal policy and income analysis than in terms of monetary policy.

CHAPTER VI

SOME IMPLICATIONS OF PUERTO RICAN EXPERIENCE

In previous chapters we have examined institutions, practices, and recent experience in Puerto Rico's external economic relations. In this chapter we wish to comment on some broader implications of the Puerto Rican experience.

ABSENCE OF A BALANCE-OF-PAYMENTS "PROBLEM"

The close similarity between an international payments system and the United States–Puerto Rican payments system has been emphasized in this study. This raises a further question: Why do balance-of-payments "problems" similar to those between nations not arise between the United States and Puerto Rico? In its economic planning the Commonwealth government rarely ever considers the possibility of any payments difficulties, and most observers assume that balance-of-payments problems cannot arise.[1] In an open economy such as Puerto Rico's, with no exchange controls and a small "foreign-exchange reserve," this view demands an explanation.

We have seen that the close links between Puerto Rico and the United States are reflected in the mechanism of income adjustment. Changes in expenditure in Puerto Rico cause changes in income and imports that quickly affect the balance of payments. Indeed, so sensitive is this mechanism that increases in Puerto Rican expendi-

---

1. "... the island can no more have a balance-of-payments problem than can an individual State of the union." Federal Reserve Bank of New York, *Monthly Review*, (April, 1960), p. 71.

tures must in a sense be "covered" by external funds before they can be made. Before the Puerto Rican banking system can expand loans, the banks must possess external funds (or assets capable of quick conversion into external funds) equal to the amount of additional loans to be made. Bank managers probably do not think about the problem in these terms, and of course their actual operations involve daily changes in asset portfolios, deposit liabilities, and mainland clearings which obscure the essential determinants of lending power, but we have seen that an increase in local loans generates changes in income and imports that quickly result in adverse external clearings approximately equal to the increase in loans.

The rapid expansion of total loans and deposits of Puerto Rican banks has been made possible by the net inflow of external capital—by the willingness of the rest of the world to hold real property and long-term claims in Puerto Rico. Without such an inflow of capital, it would be necessary for Puerto Rico to develop an export surplus on current account in order to support an increase in domestic loans and deposits.

In a sense, then, we can say that Puerto Rico has no external payments "problems" because her money supply is automatically determined by the market—the capital market and the market for goods and services. In other words, the Puerto Rican money supply is an outcome of market forces; it is not subject to conscious determination by the Commonwealth government, and that government has so far recognized and accepted its lack of autonomy in monetary policy. Not only does it lack the right to issue coin and currency (as required by the United States Constitution under present political arrangements concerning Puerto Rico), but it also makes no effort to manipulate commercial bank reserve requirements or in other ways to influence the volume of bank deposits. Consequently, it exercises no direct influence on the structure of interest rates in Puerto Rico.

These characteristics of the monetary relations between Puerto Rico and the United States suggest a further explanation for the easy and untroubled payments system that exists. The Puerto Rican economy is unlikely to be subject to the kind of instability and panic movements of capital that afflict international payments systems because the capital markets of the two regions are tightly integrated. There are many "points of contact" between the two economies. Thus Puerto Rican banks hold sizable amounts of their assets in United States securities and other claims which are readily marketable in the United States, and so do private firms and individuals. The ready market for Commonwealth government securities in New York also serves as a "point of contact." Common stock in Puerto Rican firms is not traded in great amounts in the New York market, but this is largely because such stock is closely held. Puerto Ricans, of course, hold some United States stocks and bonds. Mortgages and other forms of financial assets are marketable in mainland markets, and both banks and firms have lines of credit upon which they can draw in case of need. Banks can discount customers' paper with their mainland correspondents, while the branches of external banks can rely upon home offices for assistance. Use of a common currency in the two regions is also a point of strength, since outflows of currency provide their own exchange, so to speak. Such "points of contact" serve virtually to guarantee that, at least in the short run, payments between Puerto Rico and the mainland are not in danger of interruptions and uncertainties arising from the exchange or transfer process.

The development of a mainland market for Puerto Rican mortgages is a good illustration of the importance of institutional factors and of the way in which "local" financial claims may be transformed into "generalized" claims acceptable and readily marketable in the external world.[2] This particular illustration also involves the federal government as a supra-regional authority. Because housing mortgages in Puerto Rico are eligible for mortgage insurance under the Federal Housing Administration, it was possible for local lenders (commercial banks and other firms) to make mortgage loans for residential construction and then to sell the mortgages to mainland buyers. Although such transactions first involved FHA-insured mortgages, they were later extended to conventional mortgages as well. A large majority of mortgages financed in Puerto Rico have in fact been sold to United States buyers, and those remaining in the portfolios of local lenders can readily be sold.

Thus a large part of Puerto Rican financial claims are readily marketable in the external (mainland) financial market. Furthermore, this is more than a legal possibility; it is an actual operating practice. One can say, then, that Puerto Rican firms and the Commonwealth government can undertake anything they can finance in the New York market! We have seen that the Commonwealth government has foregone autonomy with respect to monetary policy, but this does not mean that that government cannot engage in deficit financing. As a matter of fact, outlays have regularly exceeded ordinary revenue, with the excess financed by bond issues in New York. Such bonds are sold on a competitive basis, although Puerto Rico does have the advantage (over an independent nation) that her bonds are exempt from federal income tax. This exemption of course reduces the cost of borrowing.

Through a circuitous route we come back, in a sense, to monetary policy. Through its fiscal operations the Commonwealth government does affect the insular money supply. If it borrows more heavily in New York, some portion of the "external funds" remains to support a larger volume of bank deposits, although we saw in Chapter IV

2. Cf., J. C. Ingram, "State and Regional Payments Mechanisms," *Quarterly Journal of Economics*, 73 (November, 1959), 619-32. Also, "Reply" in *Quarterly Journal of Economics*, 74 (November, 1960), 648-52.

that this portion is small. In practice, however, fiscal operations are undertaken with other objectives than monetary policy in mind. As mentioned above, changes in the money supply are simply an outcome, a by-product, and not a goal of policy. Furthermore, the Commonwealth government can do little or nothing to influence the structure of interest rates on claims that are traded in the integrated capital market. It must be a "price taker" as far as interest rates are concerned, given the quality of the security. It is in this sense that autonomy has truly been surrendered.

The Commonwealth government may in the future take a more active role in monetary policy. The Government Development Bank could begin to function as a central bank in a modest way. It could engage in open-market operations on a limited scale; it could vary collateral requirements against government deposits; and it could be given power to vary reserve requirements of Commonwealth chartered banks. However, it is likely that the government will be extremely cautious in this area. Sensitive aspects of confidence are involved, and confidence, once shaken, is not easily restored. Another possibility is that Puerto Rico will formally become part of a Federal Reserve district. This would best insure continuance of the present passive role in monetary policy.

IMPLICATIONS FOR INTERNATIONAL MONETARY POLICY

In discussions of the international monetary system and its stability, great emphasis is placed on "foreign exchange reserves." For example, the gold and dollar reserves of the United Kingdom are carefully watched and their level is treated as a vital factor in the maintenance of convertibility at a given exchange rate. In the Puerto Rican case, by contrast, no one gives much thought to the size of "external exchange reserves," and certainly the economic quantity most closely analogous to the United Kingdom reserve concept is not regarded as important in the maintenance of a smooth payments system. The reason, as we have seen, is that a wide variety of other financial claims can easily be sold abroad to increase the supply of external exchange. In the United Kingdom, on the other hand, there is a much sharper distinction between domestic and external financial instruments and claims. Emphasis is placed on the quantity of spot foreign exchange, or of assets very close to actual foreign monies such as gold and short-term treasury bills, available to monetary authorities. It is recognized that other financial claims (such as common stocks, corporate bonds, and long-term government bonds) are traded internationally, but the concern about convertibility is a concern about convertibility of *money* and the very close "near-monies." In the last few years there has indeed been a growing recognition of what might be called the convertibility of short-term securities, and it is understood that interest rates on such securities cannot vary widely without inducing a flow of transactions that tend to reduce the spread.

However, this wider concept of convertibility does not extend far into the medium-term and long-term financial instruments, nor do the actual practices of financial institutions warrant it. The risk of exchange-rate fluctuations is the major reason that a sharp line of demarcation between "domestic" and "international" (or "local" and "generalized") claims continues to exist. (Custom, lack of knowledge, and institutional inertia are other reasons.) In the absence of this risk, there is little reason to expect United Kingdom bonds to sell at a 6.5 per cent yield while United States bonds of similar maturities sell at a 3.8 per cent yield. In the case of Puerto Rico, there is no exchange-rate risk, and the concept of convertibility has extended beyond the near-monies and into the longer-term securities. Not only is $1.00 in Puerto Rico exchangeable for exactly $1.00 in New York (in a monetary sense of spot convertibility at a fixed exchange rate of unity) and a treasury bill selling at $982 in Puerto Rico also worth $982 in New York, but in addition a wider range of claims (in quality and maturity) sell for roughly equal prices (and yields) in the two markets.[3] Consequently, a shift in the external payments position of Puerto Rico is immediately accompanied by a flow of transactions in a wide range of financial instruments that serve to offset it. Thus, in sharp contrast to the United Kingdom, virtually the entire stock of financial claims in Puerto Rico can be regarded as an "external exchange reserve"; there is no reason for exclusive preoccupation with the amount of demand claims on foreigners at any moment.

This analysis has implications for some issues of international monetary policy and especially for institutional arrangements to be worked out for member nations of a common market. Current proposals to modify the international monetary system, such as those made by Triffin and Bernstein[4], place great emphasis on the size of foreign-exchange reserves and on the maintenance of convertibility of spot money and the very short-term near-monies. Triffin wants to "internationalize" exchange reserves in order to remove the danger of "hot money" movements from one currency to another. Bernstein proposes a kind of multilateral clearing agreement sponsored by the International Monetary Fund and designed to enable a single nation to receive help from others when its currency is under attack. Both of these proposals seek merely to alleviate stresses that arise when convertibility of spot money is threatened by loss of confidence in exchange-rate stability or by some change (presumably temporary) in economic conditions. Essentially, they seek to preserve the sharp separation of claims into "domestic" and "international" claims, and thus to permit a nation to determine for itself the structure of interest rates on its stock of

3. This is not to say that interest-rate differences do not arise as a result of differences in risks, imperfections of the market, and the like.

4. Robert Triffin, *Gold and the Dollar Crisis* (New Haven: Yale University Press, 1960), and E. M. Bernstein, *International Effects of U.S. Economic Policy*, Study Paper No. 16, Joint Economic Committee, 86th Cong., 2nd Sess., Jan. 25, 1960.

"domestic" claims. They recognize that in certain near-monies such a separation is no longer feasible and that short-term interest rates in the leading financial centers are linked together, but the assistance they render is to neutralize and expand exchange reserves. They do nothing to increase the number of "points of contact" or to make the total stock of claims in a nation a potential source of foreign exchange.

Other proposals and practices attempt more directly and explicitly to separate "domestic" and "international" claims. The proposal to widen the permitted range of fluctuation of a nation's exchange rate from the present 1 per cent to 5 or 10 per cent would, by increasing the risk of exchange-rate loss, widen the potential range of interest-rate differentials on short-term as well as long-term claims. If the pound sterling could vary from \$2.66 to \$2.94 (a 5 per cent range around the par of \$2.80), then no reasonable differential in the United Kingdom–United States bill rates would pull funds to London without forward-exchange cover (if the spot pound were about par). For example, if *no* variation in the spot rate were allowed, and if the market had complete confidence in the rigidly fixed rate of \$2.80 = £1, then any differential in bill rates would be erased by capital movements. If a 1 per cent exchange-rate variation were allowed, the interest-rate differential for three-month bills could be as much as 4 per cent. That is, even if the market had complete confidence in the limits (\$2.828 and \$2.772), the buyer of United Kingdom Treasury bills could lose as much as 4 per cent (annual basis) as a result of an exchange rate change. If a 5 per cent variation in the exchange rate were allowed, the interest-rate differential would have to be 20 per cent. Of course, the forward-exchange market would normally set much smaller limits to the interest-rate differential,[5] but it is nevertheless true that exchange-rate flexibility

5. Furthermore, as the spot rate approached the limits of the widened range, smaller interest-rate differentials would again become effective.

encourages a separation of national financial markets. It preserves a distinction between domestic and international financial claims. Exchange controls on capital movements are also designed to separate "domestic" from "international" claims. Finally, administrative measures such as those taken by West Germany in 1960—prohibition of interest payments on foreign-owned demand deposits, restrictions on foreign borrowing by banks and their customers—also seek to weaken the link between domestic and external interest rates. None of these administrative measures is very successful, however.

Our analysis of the Puerto Rican payments system suggests that, if nations desire to minimize payments pressures and related problems, they should seek to unify rather than separate the markets for "domestic" and "international" claims. They should take actions to extend convertibility into the longer-term financial instruments and to create a situation in which a claim of a certain maturity and risk sells at approximately the same yield (price) everywhere. Some types of claims will inevitably remain "local" in character, just as they do in Puerto Rico, but the range of "generalized" claims can certainly be greatly extended.

This suggestion means that the entire structure of interest rates in different nations would be linked together and become similar. It is often argued that this would require a supra-national body capable of determining world monetary policy and that it would mean a loss of monetary autonomy in each nation. Of course, it would mean that a nation could not fix its structure of interest rates as it chose. But a nation would still possess some control over its money supply and fiscal operations. The principal restraint would be that in financing a government deficit (or an increase in business expenditures) it would have to pay the "going" rate of interest for the type of security offered.

Our argument is that present arrangements produce

the worst results in two respects. First, efforts of nations to keep their interest rates below the going rates are a source of balance-of-payments problems for them. Such nations may try to maintain convertibility of spot monies and certain types of near-monies, but they deliberately introduce longer-term securities that are not "convertible" in the sense that they sell for the same yield as similar securities elsewhere. Not only is the nominal yield of such securities lower than that for comparable securities elsewhere, but in addition the holder bears a risk of exchange-rate change. This risk widens the perceived yield spread between domestic and foreign securities. Holders of the lower-yielding domestic securities will tend to shift toward higher-yielding foreign securities, and this shift must be checked by some form of exchange control. Thus the monetary authorities are under pressure to try to separate domestic and foreign markets for medium and long-term securities in order to preserve the yield structure of the domestic market. However, the constant inducement to shift into foreign securities, the opportunities to shift from long- to short-term domestic securities, and the ingenuity of traders faced with statutory controls, all combine to hold a steady pressure on the spot exchange rate. There is at best an uneasy equilibrium in the market for foreign exchange.

Second, institutional barriers to capital movements and the risk of exchange-rate changes serve to rob some nations (notably the United Kingdom) of the benefits of an interest-rate structure that is higher than that of external money markets. Such countries would benefit from measures that would link their capital markets more closely to external capital markets—such measures as rigidly fixed exchange rates, elimination of exchange controls, and elimination of institutional barriers to the easy flow of claims. Under present circumstances, a nation may raise its structure of interest rates considerably above those of its major trading partners (as the United Kingdom has done) only to find that the separation of its domestic capital market from foreign capital markets operates to prevent an increase in foreign purchases of its securities over a wide range of maturities. Foreign purchases tend to be concentrated in short-term securities where exchange controls are not present and where the exchange-rate risk can be covered in the forward exchange market. The higher long-term interest rates thus have their principal effect on the balance-of-payments position through indirect, slower-acting influences on domestic economic activity, rather than directly through increased foreign capital inflow. Because foreign holdings of short-term claims tend to be liquidated if and when the interest rate differential (allowing for cost of forward-exchange cover) declines, foreign purchases of such claims do not supply a permanent corrective solution. Failure to forge what we have called "points of contact" between the domestic and foreign capital markets thus exacts a penalty in instability and chronic payments pressures.

So far, nations continue to be ambivalent on this issue. There has been a vigorous movement toward convertibility of money and a recognition of intimate interconnections of short-term securities (what we have called convertibility of near-monies), but at the same time there has been a disposition to retain separate national interest-rate structures for longer-term securities and a tendency to resist a full integration of capital markets. However, the tendency of a system of fixed exchange rates and spot convertibility is toward greater "international solidarity of capital markets."[6] When this tendency is resisted, problems arise; if it were welcomed and encouraged, these problems would be abated.

It may be objected that the essential point of the foregoing discussion is simply that if there were complete confidence in the maintenance of convertibility at a fixed rate and no legal barriers to capital movements, such

6. Oskar R. Morgenstern, *International Financial Transactions* (Princeton: Princeton University Press, 1959).

movements would become quite sensitive to interest-rate differentials. Since confidence cannot be legislated, the discussion is fruitless. Our argument is that, while the matter can be put in these terms, such a formulation does not lead to a solution. The habit of thinking of two largely separate groups of financial claims—foreign-exchange reserves and mobile short-term securities, and a large mass of "domestic" claims—reduces the prospects that many interlocking points of contact will be forged between a nation's capital market and external capital markets. We saw that Puerto Rico has many such points of contact. As a result, the volume of gross capital flows is very large. Our estimates in Chapter II indicated that such flows were three times the value of total imports of goods and services, and twice as large as gross insular product. Changes in the relative structure of interest rates that influence the motivations for these capital-account transactions could enable substantial shifts in the net flow to be accommodated. We maintain that adoption of policies deliberately designed to lead toward a tighter integration of international capital markets would result in a lessening of pressures on traditional foreign-exchange reserves and in alleviation of balance-of-payments crises.

This discussion applies particularly to nations whose economies are linked closely together in world markets. We have in mind especially economic relations among members of the European common market and between the United States and Canada. It is in this context that the above remarks are most relevant. In these areas great strides have been taken toward the integration of markets for goods and services and toward freedom of certain types of factor movements. For external residents, convertibility on current account and freedom of short-term capital transactions (in some cases) have been accepted. Yet the implications of these moves for the further integration of capital markets seem not to be understood. There is still a tendency to maintain separate national markets in which an individual nation can adopt its own monetary policy in the sense of fixing its own interest-rate structure.[7] Not even the failure of exchange restrictions to control short-term capital movements has had the effect on policy one would have expected.

One consequence of the reluctance of nations to move toward full integration of capital markets is a tendency to seek solutions for payments pressures in enlarged international reserves. Emphasis is usually placed upon the cover for short-term liabilities to external residents. To protect the spot exchange rate from shifts of funds from one national currency to another, various schemes have been put forward to enlarge the stock of international reserves and to make this stock available to the country whose currency is under attack. Given the drive toward other aspects of economic integration, however, these schemes do not meet the real issue. The clue lies in their almost exclusive emphasis upon *external* liabilities. If full convertibility of spot monies is allowed (as in the United States and as approximated in some European countries), holders of the entire stock of money in a country may conceivably seek to convert their holdings into another currency. Furthermore, holders of any assets, long- or short-term, may seek to sell the assets to obtain money that will then be eligible for conversion. Attempts to meet such a threat by enlarging international reserves would be futile. There is little prospect of creating a sufficient volume of official reserves to allow conversion of any significant fraction of domestic claims into foreign monies. The real solution must be to let asset prices fall in the country concerned until they become attractive to

7. No doubt the interwar experience is responsible for the tenacity with which governments cling to autonomy in this respect. Keynes's oft-quoted speech to the House of Lords (May 23, 1944) is characteristic: ". . . we intend to retain control of our domestic rate of interest, so that we can keep it as low as suits our own purposes, without interference from the ebb and flow of international capital movements or flights of hot money." Reprinted in S. E. Harris, ed., *The New Economics* (New York: Alfred A. Knopf, 1947), p. 374.

foreign buyers (and domestic holders), at which point any further sales for the purpose of obtaining money to use in buying foreign exchange would be matched by sales of foreign exchange as foreigners begin to buy the assets in question.

Of course it is true that external holders are more likely to shift funds from domestic into foreign currency than are domestic holders, but this is a matter of degree. Furthermore, behavior patterns can change in this respect. As investment institutions, corporate treasurers, and even individuals become more sophisticated and knowledgeable about international financial transactions, their responses to price and interest differentials will probably become more sensitive. There is evidence that they have already learned much about the market for short-term securities. Further steps toward economic integration, as are contemplated in the common market, are likely to lead to more knowledge about the securities of different nations and to closer contacts through the financial markets.

A considerable amount of financial integration has already occurred in Europe. We cannot discuss this matter in detail, but a few remarks may be pertinent. Direct investment has been *de facto* free since December, 1957, when OEEC countries agreed to allow all payments "in connection with the making and the liquidation of direct investments."[8] The right to refuse permission is retained, but it is rarely used. Portfolio investment has been liberalized but not yet freed. In addition to changes in governmental regulations, there have been private and institutional developments that contribute to integration of capital markets. For example, European stock exchanges are attempting to work out standard procedures for security transactions and to increase the flow of information about corporate operations.[9] They recognize that

8. OEEC, *Liberalization of Current Invisibles and Capital Movements*, March, 1961, p. 32.

9. Representatives of eighteen stock exchanges in thirteen countries met in London in October, 1961, to discuss ways to facilitate freer movements of securities throughout Western Europe. *The Economist* (October, 14, 1961), pp. 161-62.

the traditional scarcity of published information about company accounts hinders the movement of securities. Stocks are being listed on two or more exchanges; bonds are being issued more frequently in external capital markets.

The Bank for International Settlements has called attention to the increasing financial integration of Europe and its consequences. Speaking of the years 1957 to 1960, the bank's *Annual Report* stated: "There seems to have been a tendency for long-term rates [of interest] gradually to move together—a tendency which, on account of the greater freedom of long-term capital movements between countries, can perhaps be expected to continue."[10]

If governments take steps to encourage or even allow the integration of capital markets, this tendency will continue. One consequence, we argue, is that payments pressures in the usual sense will be diminished. The role of conventional exchange reserves will be smaller, and more of the adjustment process will be accomplished through capital transactions in a wide range of securities.

We have also argued that this easy flow of capital will be facilitated by rigidly fixed exchange rates. The basis for this argument is primarily institutional, not theoretical. Banks, insurance companies, and other institutional investors are more likely to be willing to hold securities of several nations under a fixed rather than under a variable exchange rate system. And, what may be even more pertinent, they are more likely to be *permitted* such diversification by regulatory authorities in the case of fixed rates. It is true that the forward exchange market could conceivably provide almost the same assurance of reconversion into domestic currency, but there are formidable practical difficulties to the development of such a forward exchange market. For example, if a French insurance company buys a thirty-year German bond, it must make forward exchange contracts for sixty semi-annual interest pay-

10. *Thirtieth Annual Report*, Bank for International Settlements (Basle, 1960), p. 14.

ments in addition to a contract for the final redemption value of the bond. If its situation changes and it disposes of the bond before maturity, some of these contracts would have to be bought out or re-negotiated. At the very least, the necessity to cover with forward exchange contracts would reduce flexibility. Another problem concerns perpetual bonds and common stocks. How could the buyer hedge his foreign-exchange risk in these cases?

Our proposal requires that nations undertake to fix their exchange rates permanently at a given level. With the reminder that we are discussing a group of nations with a considerable degree of economic integration, such as the common market group, we shall comment briefly on the methods that might be used to fix exchange rates in this fashion. With respect to fiscal operations of governments, each nation must finance any excess of expenditures over ordinary revenues by issuing securities of suitable maturities and yields to make them salable in external capital markets. As a corollary, the prices of outstanding government securities must move to whatever levels are necessary to make them salable (marginally) in external markets. A government can still engage in deficit financing, but it must pay an interest rate high enough to compete with other issues in world capital markets. New issues of government securities might still be sold largely in the domestic market, just as in the United States the bonds of state governments are sometimes purchased by institutions and individuals within that state, although the yields must still be competitive. Similarly, in the private sector some securities would acquire the character of "generalized claims," whether because of a governmental guarantee (as with FHA-insured mortgages) or international reputation of a company (as with AT&T bonds, to take just one example), and these securities would sell for similar prices and yields in several national capital markets. Other types of claims, such as personal loans and localized debts, would continue to vary in yields from one country to another.

When the demand for foreign exchange increased, banks would be obliged to sell part of their assets in external financial markets or to discount securities with foreign banks in order to raise additional foreign exchange. Alternatively, they could simply sell securities in the domestic financial market. Such sales would marginally depress prices and raise yields of the whole range of "generalized claims" and thereby induce an increase in the supply of foreign exchange. Once the prices of securities had been equalized in domestic and external markets, very small changes in price would be sufficient to induce the necessary response.

The changes in institutions and governmental policies that would be necessary to make this system work would take some time to become effective. The transitional process would be easiest if several countries moved to adopt it at the same time, and most difficult if a single country adopted it. We shall not discuss the political aspects of the system, but these are obviously of great significance. (The reader can imagine the Congressional response had the United States Treasury begun in 1958-60 to sell refunding issues in Europe at yields necessary to attract buyers, perhaps even denominating the issues in foreign currencies.)

In order to encourage the development of numerous contacts between domestic and foreign financial markets, it would be desirable to encourage commercial banks to arrange their own facilities for settling checks drawn upon them and deposited in foreign banks. Commercial banks could arrange matching correspondent balances, set up lines of credit, work out procedures for discounting claims, and include internationally marketable claims among their assets. It goes without saying that banks should not be hampered by exchange controls on such transactions—nor, for that matter, should other traders. Other financial institutions should be encouraged to hold a wider variety of securities of different nations. In capital-short regions, where interest rates on local claims were relatively high, a mechanism would probably develop whereby these claims would be marketed in regions with more abundant capital, much as has been done for residential mortgages by mortgage companies in the United States.

Such an extension of convertibility into a wide variety of securities would reduce the concentration of pressure on the central bank and on the exchange reserves (narrowly defined) of a nation. A large part of the entire stock of claims within a national economy would become a potential source of foreign exchange. It is this broadening of the range of convertibility that could free a nation from the preoccupation with official exchange reserves that has dominated recent discussions of the international monetary system. Our argument is that this present emphasis on official short-term claims on (and liabilities to) foreigners, with its tendency to lead to a search for ways to preserve the separation of domestic and external financial markets, conflicts with the trend toward economic integration and hampers movement toward a fundamental solution to international payments problems.

These proposals for a more complete integration of financial markets raise questions about the role of central banks in such a system. Some writers have said that financial integration will require close coordination of national monetary authorities and perhaps even the creation of a supra-national monetary authority. We shall not attempt a detailed discussion of this matter, but a few remarks need to be made. First, as already mentioned, a given central bank would be unable to fix the nation's interest-rate structure at a level that differed much from levels elsewhere. Although some may regard this as a drastic surrender of autonomy, it can be argued that in nations whose economies are closely integrated the central banks do not have this power anyway. As the United Kingdom has learned, domestic interest rates cannot be set by domestic economic considerations alone. Even the United States is finding that a low long-term interest rate will lead to foreign bond issues in New York and thus accentuate balance-of-payments difficulties. It is now generally recognized that short-term rates cannot be fixed in disregard of comparable rates elsewhere. Under the present system, nations suffer the disadvantages of interdependence of interest-rate structures but do not enjoy the benefits of sensitive, equilibrating capital movements.

Second, central banks would still have some important functions to perform. They could do much to facilitate equilibrating flows of capital, and they could assist commercial banks in setting up clearing mechanisms. Their own asset portfolios could be used to generate a supply of (or demand for) foreign exchange. Through open-market operations the central bank could induce a flow of funds in the desired direction. Some scope for determination of the national money supply would also remain. The central bank could bring about marginal changes in domestic interest rates—it could slightly increase such rates in order to attract external funds, thus increasing the domestic money supply. It could also establish a system to market local claims in external markets, and by varying the volume of such transactions, it could exert some influence on the availability of credit. Variations in required reserve ratios could also furnish some degree of control.

Third, a nation would still be able to influence domestic economic activity through fiscal policy. Provided that an excess of outlays over ordinary revenues was financed by debt instruments salable in world markets, deficit financing would be feasible. Through fiscal policy the money supply would also be affected. A nation could undertake anything it could finance in the world capital market, just as Puerto Rico can undertake anything it can finance in the New York capital market. These matters need not be determined for the entire group of nations by a central authority, but each nation would be subject to a monetary discipline.

Fourth, there still remains the question of the method through which the international interest rate structure would be determined. Ideally, an international monetary authority would determine the appropriate over-all supply of money and level of interest rates. Such an authority does not now exist, however, and these matters are resolved in some way by the actions of separate national authorities. We may argue that the proposals made here do not change the present method of determination in any fundamental sense. They may create more pressures for the development of an international body, but assuming that it will not be established under the present system, the proposed system can operate under existing arrangements just as well as can the present system. In other words, the problem of regulating a world monetary policy does not arise as a result of the integration of financial markets. It was there all the time. We conclude that the proposals made here do not absolutely require the creation of a supra-national monetary authority to which national autonomy would be surrendered. The need for such an authority would be no more imperative than it is under the present system, but the need might be more clearly seen.

What we propose essentially involves the creation and acceptance of a one-price system for claims. Economic integration of national economies is usually understood to involve movement toward free trade in commodities, one result of which is a one-price system for commodities, after allowing for transport costs. So far, however, nations have tried to couple one-price commodity markets with a variable-price market for claims. This creates a great many strains, as might be expected. After all, transactions in claims are usually several times as large as transactions in commodities. In the Puerto Rican case, we estimated that gross capital movements were three times the value of gross imports. Claims of similar quality (maturity, interest rate, degree of risk) are almost perfect substitutes for each other. They are available in standard units, they are easily identifiable, and costs of transfers are small. Consequently, the demand for claims held by any one country would be highly elastic. If international transactions in claims were free from all controls, the demand and supply of foreign exchange would also be highly elastic. Such high elasticities would make for easy adjustment to any change in circumstances.

We do not argue that financial integration in the above sense would solve all problems of balance-of-payments adjustment. Difficult and painful adjustments would still be necessary, especially in the long run. Short-run payments pressures should be greatly eased, however, and attention could be shifted from the problems of short-term liquidity and the volume of international reserves to the more basic problems of resource allocation and economic efficiency. Freedom of capital movements might help to solve these problems, but we do not claim it would be sufficient. Depressed areas remain a problem even in a single country.

CHAPTER VII

SOME IMPLICATIONS FOR ECONOMIC DEVELOPMENT

Puerto Rico's remarkably successful developmental record since 1947 has attracted much attention. The annual rate of increase in gross insular product has averaged 7.7 per cent from 1947 to 1960, and the gross insular product in 1960 was 2.55 times as large as in 1947. Per capita gross product rose from $286 in 1947 to $677 in 1960. (These comparisons are in terms of current dollars. For more details see Table 11.) The ratio of gross domestic investment to gross insular product ranged from 14.3 to 22.2 per cent during this period, and Puerto Rico attracted a large inflow of mainland capital and entrepreneurship. This growth record compares favorably with records established in other rapidly growing economies, such as Canada in 1900-13, Japan in 1880-1920, and Germany after World War II.

While it is not the purpose of this study to analyze Puerto Rican economic development, the obvious importance of external trade to that development impels us to comment on it. Puerto Rico is indeed an example *par excellence* of the comparative-advantage approach to development. New investments have been strongly oriented toward export markets, especially private investment in productive facilities. Public investments have also been designed to support and encourage the expansion of export industries, although they have served the domestic sectors as well.

In considering whether or not to establish a given plant

in Puerto Rico, the size of the domestic market has not been a dominant factor, either to private entrepreneurs or to government promotional agencies. The immense market of the United States mainland is assumed to be available, and most emphasis is placed upon supply factors. (However, when the output of one industry forms the input of another, as in the petro-chemical complex, the size of domestic demand becomes an important factor. This is a question of industrial balance, however, and the market for *final* product is still primarily an external one.)

One result (and indication) of the export orientation of Puerto Rican development has been an increase in the relative importance of foreign trade in the economy. The usual experience, even in countries whose economies are heavily dependent on foreign trade, is that the ratios of exports and imports to gross product decline in the course of development. In Puerto Rico, however, these ratios have risen as follows:

Ratio	*Per Cent*	
	1947	*1960*
Merchandise Exports/Gross Insular Product	31.8	41.1
Merchandise Imports/Gross Insular Product	53.1	59.2
Current Account Credits/Gross Insular Product	47.6	57.8
Current Account Debits/Gross Insular Product	68.1	76.5

We should mention that these very large ratios of trade to gross product are exaggerated by the role of re-exports. This matter was discussed in Chapter V, where rough estimates were made of the value of imports entering into exports.

IS PUERTO RICO A SPECIAL CASE?

The remarkable progress of the Puerto Rican economy since World War II is often attributed to certain unique advantages enjoyed by Puerto Rico, and it is argued that her experience is not particularly relevant to the problems of other, less fortunately situated, underdeveloped countries. The most important of Puerto Rico's allegedly unique advantages are the following:

1. Because of her status as an integral part of the United States economy, her exports to the mainland are free of duties or other restrictions.

2. Because of her special status as a Commonwealth, Puerto Rico is not subject to federal income or excise taxes. Therefore, when the Puerto Rican government grants new firms an exemption from Puerto Rican taxes, the inducement to direct investment is extremely powerful.

3. Because Puerto Rico is a part of the United States, Puerto Ricans are citizens of the United States, and constitutional guarantees of civil and property rights are fully applicable. This means that workers may move freely to and from the United States labor market and that owners of capital need have little fear of political instability.

Other significant advantages are that Puerto Rico does not have to provide for her own defense forces, that she receives large unilateral transfers from the federal government, and that she possessed, in 1947, a sizable war-accumulated grubstake of liquid assets, which she did not squander but wisely employed in launching her developmental program.

These advantages have certainly played an important role in Puerto Rico's recent development. They have served to facilitate and stimulate both government and private enterprise.

After an early, ambitious beginning, the government chose to concentrate on the provision of power, transportation, water supply, education, and other types of social overhead investment. Because interest on their bonds is exempt from federal income taxes to United States residents, the Commonwealth government and public authorities are able to borrow in the New York market at relatively low rates of interest. Commonwealth bonds have sold since 1947 at yields comparable to those of high quality state and municipal bonds.

Availability of external capital for social overhead investment at such low rates of interest has been another important advantage to Puerto Rico. The low rates of interest have helped to hold down the cost of electric power, water, and other services provided by the government and its semi-autonomous authorities. Lower prices for these services increase the profitability of private business and thus help to attract new firms. The Commonwealth government has carefully guarded and nurtured its credit rating in the New York capital market. It operates within a limit on debt-incurring capacity; it abides by the exact terms of sinking fund and other provisions of the bond contract; and its public authorities have operated with a comfortable margin of net income over debt service requirements. As a result, Commonwealth bonds enjoy a high credit rating, and the Commonwealth government has access to *private* external capital at a much lower cost than has any other underdeveloped country.

Although Puerto Rico has sought to minimize the cost of external capital used by the government, it has not tried to place any limit on the rates of return earned by external investors in Puerto Rican industry. Indeed, in its efforts to attract private direct investment and entrepreneurship, the Commonwealth government has done much to increase the profitability of such investment. The ten-year tax exemption program is well known, but the Economic Development Administration provides many other forms of assistance to prospective firms. We shall not describe this program here, but descriptive literature is readily available.

The point we wish to emphasize is that Puerto Rican authorities have not been concerned about high rates of return on external direct investment. They have not believed that high profits are detrimental to the Puerto Rican economy, and they have not had any fear of a "transfer problem" or other difficulties in the balance of payments that might be associated with the remission of profits earned. Puerto Rican officials have in fact emphasized that their experience has shown that very high prospective rates of return on investment are necessary to induce firms to establish plants in Puerto Rico. They have sometimes shocked their Latin American colleagues at international conferences by suggesting that rates of return on equity investment may have to be 50 to 100 per cent per year in order to attract external capital.

The fact is that, despite the favorable operating experiences of plants owned by the United States in Puerto Rico, vigorous promotional efforts are still necessary to maintain the rate of capital inflow, and extraordinary incentives still seem necessary. H. C. Barton has noted that: "Ever since the number of Fomento firms has been large enough for meaningful comparison with U. S. manufacturing experience, their profits have been twice as high in relation to equity investment . . . as companies in the same asset size classes in the United States, *before* taxes."[1] Barton finds it puzzling that this differential return alone does not suffice to attract a great many firms to Puerto Rico, but it apparently does not. When tax-exemption is allowed for in the experience cited above, the return on equity in Puerto Rico is *four times* as large as in the United States. In particular industries, the average rates of return on equity investment have often exceeded 50 per cent. As Barton says, the wonder is that the flow of capital to Puerto Rico has not been much greater than it has been.

To illustrate the profitability of some Puerto Rican operations, we give below some financial data for five firms engaged in the manufacture of household appliances. While this is not an average or typical experience, it does dramatize the potential profitability of Puerto Rican

1. H. C. Barton, Jr., "Puerto Rico's Industrial Development Program, 1942-1960," a paper presented at the Center for International Affairs, Harvard University, October 29, 1959.

plants. For the fiscal year ending June 30, 1958, the five firms reported income as follows:

Household Appliances
Condensed Income Statement[2]

Sales Receipts		$18,885,000
Other Income		78,000
		$18,963,000
Less: Payroll	2,066,000	
Other Costs	7,547,000	−9,613,000
	Profit	$ 9,350,000

The ratio of profit to sales was 49.5 per cent; the ratio of payroll to sales was 10.9 per cent. These firms import components, assemble them with low-wage Puerto Rican labor, and re-export the finished products to the mainland. Since they pay no taxes in Puerto Rico (as yet), their principal impact on the domestic economy is through their employment of domestic labor.

Although these firms have a rather small impact on the Puerto Rican economy, it seems clear that their net impact is desirable and that the high rate of profit is not harmful even if fully remitted. The sales of these firms generate the external funds required to cover both imported materials and remission of profits. When tax exemption expires, the firms will (if their profits remain high) begin to make substantial contributions to the Puerto Rican treasury.[3]

2. *Annual Statistical Report of EDA Manufacturing Plants*, Commonwealth of Puerto Rico, Economic Development Administration, 1958-59 ed.

3. Consistency and accuracy of accounting procedures assumes a critical importance in these matters. While tax exemption is in force, the firms have an incentive to underprice the imported materials and overprice the exports, thus maximizing the tax-exempt Puerto Rican profit. The U.S. Treasury Department is alert to this problem. When tax exemption ends, the Commonwealth Treasury will not want to see the pricing policies changed to reduce the profit on Puerto Rican operations. When the Puerto Rican plant is a branch or subsidiary of a U.S. firm, as it often is, the inherent difficulties of insuring consistent and fair methods in intra-firm accounting pose critical problems.

Actually, these firms have chosen to retain most of their profits in Puerto Rico. This is a common practice of direct investment companies, and the reason is that such profits are subject to United States corporate or individual income taxes when remitted. This fact may ultimately lead to reinvestment of accumulated profits in Puerto Rico, thus providing an "internal" supply of investible funds. So far, however, many firms are simply accumulating liquid assets. This is what our household appliance firms are doing, as is indicated by the following remarkable balance sheet:

Household Appliances[4]
Balance Sheet as of June 30, 1958

Assets		Liabilities and Net Worth	
Cash and Receivables	$19,179,000	Accounts and Notes Payable	$ 36,000
Inventories	2,019,000	Other Liabilities	16,000
Land and Depreciated Assets	2,638,000	Earned Surplus	21,964,000
Other Assets	564,000	Capital Stock and Paid-in Surplus	1,070,000
	$24,400,000		$24,400,000

These plants had been in operation for an average of 3.3 years at the end of fiscal year 1958; in that period they had accumulated nearly $22 million of earned surplus, after having started with $1 million of paid-in capital. The accumulated earnings were being held in cash and receivables, giving these firms what must surely be one of the highest current ratios on record. In reporting the rate of return on capital, the EDA report calculates the ratio of profits to total assets (38.3 per cent) and profit to average equity including accumulated earnings (43.4 per cent). A more relevant measure is the ratio of profit to *employed*

4. *Annual Statistical Report of EDA Manufacturing Plants.*

capital, thus omitting most of the cash and receivables. Assuming that $500,000 in cash would be sufficient for operating requirements, we estimate the amount of capital employed to be $5.7 million. On this basis, the ratio of profit to capital is 164 per cent. Since the income is tax exempt, the rate of profit certainly compares favorably with United States after-tax experience!

Although we have chosen an extreme example to illustrate the profit potential in Puerto Rican investment, the experience of the household appliance firms is by no means unique. Firms in some other industries have performed as well. Indeed, for 415 EDA-promoted manufacturing plants (omitting only the petroleum refining industry), the average rate of profit on our concept of *employed* capital was 27 per cent in 1958. Earned surplus was over twice the paid-in capital, and cash and receivables approximately equaled the amount of earned surplus.

Thus, while Puerto Rico has obtained capital for public investment at low rates of interest, she has not balked at high rates of return on private direct investment. In many countries, such high rates of profit would be attacked as harmful to the national economy and as a hindrance to its economic development. In Puerto Rico, however, this view is conspicuously absent.

Our answer to the initial question in this section is that some of Puerto Rico's advantages are relative rather than unique and that Puerto Rican experience cannot be dismissed as a special case without relevance for other underdeveloped countries. For example, the fact that Puerto Rican exports enter the United States market duty-free is not a decisive advantage because United States tariffs are not high on most commodities that are likely to be imported from underdeveloped countries. The difference between a zero duty and a 10 or 20 per cent duty may be offset by other advantages of the underdeveloped country (such as lower money wages). A more important matter than the level of duties is assurance of continued access to the United States market. It is in this sense that Puerto Rico does have a unique advantage. Other countries face the risk of escape-clause action or other administrative actions designed to limit their access to the United States market; Puerto Rican access is guaranteed by existing legislation and constitutional provisions. This is certainly a powerful advantage, as it removes an element of risk in the estimation of demand by potential investors.

Tax exemption has also been important in Puerto Rican development. However, this is a device that could be used by other underdeveloped countries as well. That is, any country could exempt newly established plants from corporate income taxes for a period of years, just as Puerto Rico has done. United States firms could set up branches or subsidiaries in such countries and avoid federal income taxes until profits were remitted to the United States. In this respect Puerto Rico has no unique advantage.

The third Puerto Rican advantage mentioned above may well be the most important—namely, the political stability resulting from United States constitutional guarantees. This provides an element of confidence to potential investors that can scarcely be matched by any other country. Even here, however, if a country wished to follow the Puerto Rican pattern it could take many steps to create an investment climate favorable to foreign capital. Creation of such a climate, coupled with United States governmental guarantees against certain investment risks, would approach if not equal the Puerto Rican situation.

Another Puerto Rican advantage, access to private United States capital for social overhead investment at low rates of interest, is partially offset in that other countries have access to loans from the World Bank and from various governmental lending agencies such as the Export-Import Bank and the Inter-American Development ment Bank. They are also eligible for outright grants of economic aid.

Finally, it is a significant fact that practially all of the present Puerto Rican advantages existed in the period before 1947, but that she had very little economic development (except for the wartime boom) until the vigorous Fomento program began in the postwar period. Even though Puerto Rico has followed the comparative advantage path, much credit for her achievements in the last fifteen years must go to the conscious development policies of the Commonwealth government, policies designed and administered to foster the growth of private investment along with rapid expansion of public investment in social overhead facilities. The Puerto Rican record illustrates both the efficacy of active governmental intervention and the power of private enterprise.

A PESSIMISTIC VIEW OF PUERTO RICAN EXPERIENCE

Even though we have argued that Puerto Rican advantages are a matter of degree, and that Puerto Rican experience does contain some useful lessons for other underdeveloped countries, there are also grounds for pessimism in the Puerto Rican record.

First, it is significant that Puerto Rican investment has been almost wholly financed from external sources. That is, the current account deficit in the balance of payments has been approximately equal to gross insular investment for the period 1947 to 1960 (see Table 17). Despite the substantial rise in per capita income, domestic savings have not risen enough to furnish a significant amount of funds for expansion of investment. Since other countries cannot depend entirely on capital inflows, they must find some means of inducing domestic savings.

Second, the curious employment experience of Puerto Rico is not encouraging. Despite the huge net capital inflow, which amounted to over $1,000 *per capita*[5] for the

5. This estimate is obtained by dividing aggregate current-account deficits for 1947-60 by the average population for the period. Thus we are treating as capital inflow not only the capital transactions themselves but also unilateral transfers, remittances, and the disposition of Puerto Rico's wartime accumulation of external assets.

entire period, 1947 to 1960, total employment actually declined from 1947 to 1960! Total employment was about 600,000 in 1947, and it fell to 543,000 in 1960. The net capital inflow (current account deficit) was $2,580,000,000 for these fourteen years, an amount equal to about $4,600 per employed worker in the same period. Nevertheless, total employment declined over this period, unemployment remained at about the same level, and the population pressure was largely neutralized by the migration of Puerto Ricans to the United States. The pertinent figures are as follows:[6]

	Population	Labor Force	Employed	Unemployed
1950	2,207,000	686,000	596,000	88,000
1960	2,337,000	625,000	543,000	82,000

This curious and surprising employment experience can be emphasized by comparing actual figures for 1960 with the careful projections made by Harvey Perloff in the late 1940's. Perloff's projections are published in his book, *Puerto Rico's Economic Future*.[7] (It should be noted that we imply no criticism of Perloff's estimates in making these comparisons. His assumptions were eminently sensible at the time.) Perloff's conservative (low) estimate of population in 1960 was 2,678,000, out of which he expected a labor force of 846,000. The actual population in 1960 was 2,337,000, the labor force only 625,000. The estimated and actual employment by industry was as follows:[8]

6. *Economic Report to the Governor, 1960*, Commonwealth of Puerto Rico, Planning Board, Table 31. Exactly comparable 1947 figures are not available, but in the several sources there is agreement that employment fell from 1947 to 1960.

7. Harvey Perloff, *Puerto Rico's Economic Future* (Chicago: University of Chicago Press, 1950), especially Chapter 19.

8. Actual figures are from *Economic Report to the Governor, 1960*. Perloff's estimates are from *Puerto Rico's Economic Future*, pp. 252-53.

Industry	Perloff Estimate for 1960	Actual 1960
Agriculture, Fishing, Mining	250,000	127,000
Manufacturing	200,000	92,000
Services	350,000	324,000
Employed	800,000	543,000
Unemployed	46,000	82,000
TOTAL LABOR FORCE	846,000	625,000

Perloff leaned toward the conservative end of his range for population and labor force estimates, but he recognized that it would be difficult to achieve the large increase in employment represented by the above figures. He estimated that gross investment of $85 million per year (not including agriculture) would be required, most of which would have to come from external sources. This was seen to be a formidable goal. However, as it happened, gross insular investment averaged $194 million per year from 1947 to 1960, more than twice Perloff's estimate.[9] As already mentioned, nearly all of this investment was financed externally in the sense that current account deficits almost equaled gross insular investment. Public and private consumption were almost equal to gross insular product.

Thus we see that the massive capital inflow into Puerto Rico did not even maintain the level of employment, much less absorb and utilize the labor-force increase associated with a rising population. Emigration of Puerto Ricans to the United States prevented a sharp increase in unemployed. *Net* emigration in the period 1947 to 1960 totaled 581,000, a number greater than total employment in Puerto Rico in 1960.[10] Even so, unemployment remained

9. See Table 17. Perloff's estimate was based on 1948 prices. Allowance for price changes would reduce our figure of $194 million to about $170 million.

10. *Statistical Yearbook, Historical Statistics, 1959,* Commonwealth of Puerto Rico, Planning Board, p. 218; and *Economic Report to the Governor, 1960,* Table 20.

at 12 to 15 per cent of the labor force. (Net emigration of course includes women, children, and other persons not in the labor force, but males between fifteen and forty-nine have predominated, especially in recent years.)

Puerto Rico's employment experience makes unpleasant reading for densely populated underdeveloped countries who have little prospect of equaling her rate of investment, whether from external or domestic resources, and who also have no outlet in emigration for a growing population. With all her advantages and for all her notable achievements, Puerto Rico's performance still falls short of what must be accomplished in many underdeveloped countries. (The Indian case comes immediately to mind. Through the First and Second Five-year Plans, the increase in employment did not keep up with growth in the labor force, and unemployment continued to increase.) In most underdeveloped countries, private capital movements plus governmental loans and grants are measured in cents per capita, not in hundreds or thousands of dollars.

Several reasons for Puerto Rico's employment experience have been offered. We will mention a few of them, but our discussion will be quite brief.

1. The agricultural sector evidently concealed much underemployment and seasonal unemployment of labor in 1947. As opportunities in other sectors appeared, many persons supposedly employed in agriculture were induced to change occupation. Such shifts leave the employment totals unchanged, but in a sense the real level of employment has risen.

2. The largest single manufacturing industry in 1947 was home needlework, organized on a putting-out system. Employment in this industry fell from 51,000 in 1950 to 10,000 in 1960, largely as a result of the imposition of modest wage minimums.

3. As incomes increased, many housewives and other persons withdrew from the labor force. Of persons aged

fourteen and over, the fraction in the labor force fell from 55 per cent in 1950 to 45 per cent in 1960.

4. The administration of minimum wage laws in Puerto Rico has served to restrain the growth of employment in covered industries. This point applies to both federal and Commonwealth minima, but especially to the former. Broadly speaking, federal minimum-wage boards have made it their policy to increase the minimum wage in each industry to as high a level as would be consistent with no *decline* in employment in that industry. (The home needlework case is a dramatic exception.)

This question has been closely studied within the Puerto Rican government.[11] Here we wish only to point out that the policy has obviously limited the expansion of employment in covered industries. It restricts employment in existing plants, and it lessens the incentive to establish new plants.

5. Finally, we should note that a marked upgrading of the Puerto Rican labor force has occurred since 1947. This point is implicit in (1) and (2) above, but it is important enough to be mentioned again. It is emphasized in a recent study of this and related problems, *Unemployment, Family Income, and Level of Living in Puerto Rico*,[12] in which changes in the structure of employment are analyzed. The interesting point is made that unemployed persons in Puerto Rico typically do not belong to the lowest income-class of *families*. Unemployed persons are members of families one or more of whose members already hold relatively good jobs; therefore, they can afford to remain unemployed rather than to accept an undesirable job.

A third reason for pessimism about Puerto Rican ex-

11. See especially the paper by H. C. Barton, Jr., and Robert A. Solo, both then in the Economic Development Administration, "The Effect of Minimum Wage Laws on the Economic Growth of Puerto Rico," a paper presented at the Center for International Studies, Harvard University, October, 1959 (mimeographed).

12. Committee on Human Resources, Commonwealth of Puerto Rico (undated but released in 1960).

perience is that her rapid rise in income and urbanization has not reduced the rate of population growth very considerably. The birth rate fell from 43 to 32 per 1,000 between 1947 to 1960, but the death rate fell from 12 to 7 per 1,000, and population would still be growing 2.5 per cent per year if it were not for emigration.

Our conclusion is that Puerto Rican economic development is not a unique case, of little relevance to other underdeveloped countries. Even though relevant, the Puerto Rican record may make dismal reading for other countries. Although she has had few balance-of-payments difficulties, Puerto Rico has had plenty of other problems. Other countries can expect to share most Puerto Rican problems, but they cannot expect to share all of her advantages. In particular, other countries cannot expect to receive massive inflows of capital, nor will they be able to export population growth, nor will they have such an easy and assured access to mass markets for new output.

INDEX

Accounting framework, 34-44

Alaska, 4

Balance of payments, relation to gross flow of funds, 9, 13-14, 23-24; capital account of, 9, 23, 63-65, 70-72, 75-76, 93-94, 124; current account of, 23, 59-63, 65-66, 70-72, 75-76, 93-94, 103-10, 143; response to an inflow of capital, 48-57, 81-112 *passim*; adjustment problems and crises in, 55-58, 113-17, 122-25, 130; Puerto Rican experience with, in postwar period, 57-80 *passim*; treatment of federal transactions in, 59n, 64-65; implications of Puerto Rican experience for customs union, 117-33; relation to gross insular product, 135; mentioned, 4, 6, 19, 133, 148. *See also* Capital movements, Unilateral transfers

Bank for International Settlements, 127

Bonds. *See* Securities

Branches and subsidiaries of mainland firms, 12, 28, 36n, 139n

Capacity effects, 103, 105-12

Capital, 93, 140-41. *See also* Investment

Capital movements, short-term, 14, 23-24, 26, 60-61, 66-67, 75, 124; long term, 23-24, 26, 48, 52, 61, 66, 69-70, 72, 75, 93-94, 114, 126-27; effect on income and balance of payments, 48-57, 81-112 *passim*; postwar experience in Puerto Rico, 58-61, 66-72, 74-77, 103, 111; private, 61, 69, 72, 75, 137-41; public, 61, 69, 72, 116, 136-37; relation to changes in money supply, 87-89; exchange controls on, 121-22; institutional barriers to, 122-24, 129; European regulations concerning, 126-27; inflow per capita, postwar, 143-44; mentioned, 3, 6, 114, 133. *See also* Direct investment, Exchange reserves

Central bank, 130-31. *See also* Federal Reserve System

Clearings, 13, 27, 29-30, 36-42, 49, 51, 53, 55, 66, 114

Commercial and financial transactions, 19-21, 23-26

Commercial banks, definition of Puerto Rican, 9-10, 29-30; their role in payments process, 9-12, 21, 29-44 *passim*, 129; United States, 10, 26, 29-30, 34-44, 46-48, 51, 56, 60-61, 84n; Canadian, 10, 29-30, 56, 84n; exchange charge levied by, 11-13, 42, 85; accounts of United States Treasury Department with, 12, 27, 30-31, 37-41, 44; assets of Puerto